History of
Makkah

© Dar-us-Salam,2002
   King Fahd National Library Cataloging-in-Publication Data
Maktaba Dar-us-Salam.
   History of Makkah. - Riyadh, 2002

   176p ; 14x21cm

   ISBN: 9960-892-02-6
   1- Makkah Al Mukaramah - History   1-Title
   953. 121 dc   1423/4711

   L.D. no 1423/4711
   ISBN: 9960-892-02-6

History of
Makkah

Prepared by a Group of Scholars
Under the Supervision of
Shaikh Safiur Rahman Mubarakpuri

Translated by:
Nasiruddin al-Khattab

DARUSSALAM
GLOBAL LEADER IN ISLAMIC BOOKS

Riyadh, Jeddah, Al-Khobar, Sharjah
Lahore, London, Houston, New York

First Edition: August 2002

Supervised by:

ABDUL MALIK MUJAHID

K.S.A.
- Riyadh
  Darussalam Showroom:
  Tel 00966-1-4614483 Fax: 4644945
- Jeddah
  Darussalam Showroom:
  Tel & Fax: 00966-2-6807752
- Al-Khobar
  Darussalam Showroom:
  Tel: 00966-3-8692900
  Fax: 00966-3-8691551

U.A.E
- Darussalam, Sharjah U.A.E
  Tel: 00971-6-5632623 Fax: 5632624

Pakistan
- Darussalam, 50 Lower Mall, Lahore
  Tel: 0092-42-724 0024 Fax: 7354072
  Rahman Market, Ghazni Street
- Urdu Bazar Lahore
  Tel: 0092-42-7120054 Fax: 7320703

U.S.A
- Darussalam, Houston
  P.O Box: 79194 Tx 772779
  Tel: 001-713-722 0419
  Fax: 001-713-722 0431
  E-mail: sales@dar-us-salam.com
- Darussalam, New York
  572 Atlantic Ave, Brooklyn
  New York-11217, Tel: 001-718-625 5925

U.K
- Darussalam International Publications Ltd.
  226 High Street, Walthamstow,
  London E17 7JH, Tel: 0044-208 520 2666
  Mobile: 0044-794 730 6706
  Fax: 0044-208 521 7645
- Darussalam International Publications Limited
  Regent Park Mosque, 146 Park Road,
  London Nw8 7RG Tel: 0044-207 724 3363

France
- Editions & Librairie Essalam
  135, Bd de Ménilmontant- 75011 Paris
  Tél: 0033-01- 43 38 19 56/ 44 83
  Fax: 0033-01- 43 57 44 31
  E-mail: essalam@essalam.com

Australia
- ICIS: Ground Floor 165-171, Haldon St.
  Lakemba NSW 2195, Australia
  Tel: 00612 9758 4040 Fax: 9758 4030

Malaysia
- E&D Books SDN. BHD.-321 B 3rd Floor,
  Suria Klcc
  Kuala Lumpur City Center 50088
  Tel: 00603-21663433 Fax: 459 72032

Singapore
- Muslim Converts Association of Singapore
  32 Onan Road The Galaxy
  Singapore- 424484
  Tel: 0065-440 6924, 348 8344
  Fax: 440 6724

Sri Lanka
- Darul Kitab 6, Nimal Road, Colombo-4
  Tel: 0094-1-589 038 Fax: 0094-74 722433

Kuwait
- Islam Presentation Committee
  Enlightment Book Shop
  P.O. Box: 1613, Safat 13017 Kuwait
  Tel: 00965-244 7526, Fax: 240 0057

India
- Islamic Dimensions
  56/58 Tandel Street (North)
  Dongri, Mumbai 4000 009,India
  Tel: 0091-22-3736875, Fax: 3730689
  E-mail:sales@IRF.net

South Africa
- Islamic Da'wah Movement (IDM)
  48009 Qualbert 4078 Durban,South Africa
  Tel: 0027-31-304-6883
  Fax: 0027-31-305-1292
  E-mail: idm@ion.co.za

إِنَّ أَوَّلَ بَيْتٍ وُضِعَ لِلنَّاسِ لَلَّذِى بِبَكَّةَ مُبَارَكًا وَهُدًى لِّلْعَلَمِينَ
(آل عمران: ٩٦)

Contents

Publisher's Foreword

The importance and religious status of Makkah Al-Mukarramah

The sanctity of Makkah

The boundaries of the *Haram* (Sanctuary)

The sanctity of the *Haram*

The names of Makkah

The superiority of Makkah

Living in Makkah

Description of the Holy Ka'bah and the history of its construction and maintenance

    The construction of the Ka'bah

    How Ibrahim الليه and Isma'il الليه built the Ka'bah

    How Quraish rebuilt the Ka'bah

    The Prophet ﷺ put the Black Stone in place

    How Ibn Az-Zubair رضي rebuilt the Ka'bah

    The incident of the Elephant

    The destruction of the Ka'bah at the end of time

Custodianship of the Ka'bah

The cover of the Ka'bah

    The cover before Islam

    The covering of the Ka'bah in Islamic times

    The cover during the Saudi period

Maqam Ibrahim (the Station of Ibrahim) and its virtues

Al-Hijr

The virtues of the Black Stone

The well of Zamzam

The disappearance of Zamzam

'Abdul-Muttalib redug the well of Zamzam

The names of Zamzam

The water of Zamzam and its virtues

Zamzam is healing

And it is food

Stories of the healing of the sick with Zamzam water

Al-Multazam

The conquest of Makkah

The armies enter Makkah

The people's oath of allegiance to Allâh's Messenger ﷺ

The length of the Prophet's stay in Makkah and some of the important things that he did

The ban on the *Mushrikun* entering Al-Masjid Al-Haram

The development of Al-Masjid Al-Haram throughout the ages

The era of the Rightly-Guided Caliphs and those who came after them

The addition of 'Abdullah bin Az-Zubair ﷺ

The addition of Abu Ja'far Al-Mansur

The addition of Al-Mahdi

The addition of Dar An-Nadwah

The Gate of Ibrahim

The development of Sultan Saleem

Expansion of Al-Masjid Al-Haram during the Saudi era

Beginning of expansion

The first expansion – 1375 AH/1956 CE

The expansion of King Fahd bin 'Abdul-'Aziz Aal Sa'ud (may Allâh protect him) – 1409 AH/1988 CE

Unification of the prayer halls of the *Haram*

Historical sites in Makkah

Jabal Hira'

Jabal Thawr

Masjid Al-Khaif and its virtues

The graveyard of Al-Mu'alla

Mina

'Arafat

Muzdalifah

Al-Muhassir

Al-Muhassab

Masjid At-Tan'im

Masjid Al-Ji'ranah

Masjid Al-Jinn (the Mosque of the Jinn)

Hajj (Pilgrimage)

The *Miqats* of *Ihram*

The obligations of *Ihram*

The *Sunnahs* of *Ihram*

Hajj of a minor

Things that are prohibited during *Ihram*

The amount of the *Fidyah* (expiation or ransom)

    The penalty for hunting

    Obligation of offering the *Hady* (sacrifice) for those who are doing *Tamattu'* and *Qiran*

    The *Fidyah* to be given by one who is prevented from doing *Hajj* if he cannot find a *Hady*

    The *Fidyah* for having intercourse or doing any of the things that lead to it

The pillars and obligatory duties of *Hajj*

The pillars and obligatory duties of *'Umrah*

What the pilgrim should do when he enters Makkah

As-Safa and Al-Marwah, and the command to do *Sa'y* between them

Going out to Mina

Going out to 'Arafat

    What is meant by standing in 'Arafat

    Rulings

    The conditions of standing in 'Arafat

Departing to Muzdalifah and spending the night there

    Is anyone excused from staying overnight in Muzdalifah?

    The ruling on staying overnight in Muzdalifah

The return to Mina

The first stage of exiting *Ihram*

Tawaf Al-Ifadah

Sa'y for those who are doing *Tamattu'*

The obligation of offering a sacrifice (*Hady*) for those

doing *Tamattu'* and *Qiran*

Conditions of the *Hady*

The order of rituals on the day of Sacrifice

The second stage of exiting *Ihram*

Going back to Mina

Conditions of stoning the *Jamarat*

Some charitable institutions and universities in Makkah Al-Mukarramah

Muslim World League (*Rabitah Al-'Alam Al-Islami*)

The main bodies and councils in the Muslim World League

Charitable Organization for Memorization of the Holy Qur'ân (*Jama'ah Khairiyah li Tahfîzul-Qur'ânil-Karim*)

Ummul-Qura University (*Jami'at Ummul-Qura*)

Darul-Hadith Al-Makkiyah

Madrasah Darul-Hadith Al-Khairiyah

The most famous Libraries in Makkah Al-Mukarramah

Maktabah Al-Haram Al-Makki (Library of the Makkan Sanctuary)

Al-Maktabah Al-'Ammah (Public Library) – belonging to the Board of Education

Maktabah Jami' Al-Furqan

Maktabah Jami'at Ummul-Qura

Maktabah Makkah

Some other historical locations in Makkah Al-Mukarramah

Publishers Foreword

In the Name of Allâh,
the Most Gracious, the Most Merciful

This book sheds light on various aspects of the city of Makkah, so that when he has finished the book, the reader will have an integrated picture of this holy city.

This book is not purely historical, for we only relate here the historical events that have had a direct effect on Makkah and its development, sanctity and religious status.

The book begins with a discussion of the sacred nature of Makkah Al-Mukarramah, the boundaries of the *Haram* (Sanctuary) and its sanctity. Then it discusses the superiority of Makkah and narrates *Ahadith* to that effect. Then it mentions the names of Makkah and the significance of these names.

This book also speaks of Ibrahim (Abraham) and Isma'il (Ishmael) (peace be upon them) and their connection to Makkah and its sanctity and development. For Makkah derives its sanctity and high status from the presence of the Ka'bah in the city. An entire section of the book is devoted to the Ka'bah and discusses its origins and construction, the connection of Hajrah (Hagar) and Isma'il 'alayhis-salam to it, what has happened to it as it has been destroyed and rebuilt throughout the ages, and who its custodians have been. The book also discusses the holy places that are connected to it, such as the

Maqam (the Station of Ibrahim), *Al-Hajar Al-Aswad* (the Black Stone), Al-Hijr and Al-Multazam.

Naturally enough, the book devotes a considerable amount of attention to the well of Zamzam, describing the history of its origins, how it was re-dug, its superiority, how its water is used to treat sickness, and real-life examples of that.

Then the book discusses the conquest of Makkah and its far-reaching effects on the history of Makkah and on the future of Islam and its spread, and how the House was cleansed of *Shirk* (polytheism) and the *Mushrikun* (polytheists).

There are some important places that always come to mind when Makkah is mentioned, for they are strongly connected to it. It is essential to mention these places also which include: Hira', the mountain of Thawr, 'Arafat, Al-Muhassir, the mosque of Al-Khaif, Muzdalifah and the graveyard of Al-Mu'alla.

At the end of the book the reader will find a section devoted to discussion of *Hajj* and its rituals, because *Hajj* is strongly connected to Makkah and its sites in the minds of the Muslims.

May Allâh bless our Prophet Muhammad and all his family and Companions, and those who follow them in truth until the Day of Judgement.

Abdul-Malik Mujahid

General Manager

The Importance and Religious Status of Makkah Al-Mukarramah

In the Name of Allâh,
the Most Gracious, the Most Merciful

Makkah is the holy land, the most beloved land to Allâh and His Messenger ﷺ, the *Qiblah* (direction faced in prayer) of the Muslims, the focus of their love and the place where they come together in pilgrimage. Allâh made it sacred and bestowed respect and sanctity upon it the day He created the heavens and the earth. In it is the Ka'bah, the first House set up for the worship of Allâh on earth. For the sacred House, Allâh set up a sanctuary so that it might be venerated, in which He created safety and protection even for the trees and plants, which should not be cut down or picked, and for the birds which are not to be disturbed. He has decreed that rewards for deeds in Makkah are greater than rewards for deeds done elsewhere, and prayer in Makkah is equal to one hundred thousand prayers elsewhere. It is from the greatness and sanctity of the House that Makkah takes its greatness and sanctity; and from the security of the House, Makkah derives its security – as Allâh says:

﴿ وَمَن دَخَلَهُ كَانَ ءَامِنًا ﴾ [آل عمران:٩٧]

"...whosoever enters it, he attains security."
[*Aal 'Imran* 3:97]

Allâh swears by Makkah as an indication of its great status, as He says:

﴿ لَآ أُقْسِمُ بِهَٰذَا ٱلْبَلَدِ ﴾ [البلد:١]

"I swear by this city (Makkah)." [*Al-Balad* 90:1]

It was in Makkah that Allâh's Messenger ﷺ said:

"By Allâh, you are the best land of Allâh, the most beloved land of Allâh to Allâh. Had I not been driven out of you, I would not have left you."[1]

And it was reported that Ka'b ؓ said: "Allâh favored some lands over others, and the most beloved land to Allâh is *Al-Balad Al-Haram* (the Sacred City)."[2]

On the basis of the high status and the great esteem in which Makkah is held by Allâh, His Messenger ﷺ and all the Muslims, we have written this book, hoping that Allâh will accept it as a righteous deed and that He will benefit thereby the Muslims who read it. We have striven our utmost to report the *Sahih* (sound) *Ahadith* and the strong reports; if we have succeeded, it is by the grace and bounty of Allâh.

---

[1] *Ahmad* (4/305), *Ad-Darimi* (2513), *At-Tirmidhi* (3925) and *Ibn Majah* (3108) from 'Abdullah bin 'Adi bin Al-Hamra'. Classed as *Sahih* by Shaikh Al-Albani in *Sahih At-Tirmidhi* and *Sahih Ibn Majah*.

[2] Part of a lengthy narration reported by Al-Baihaqi in *Ash-Shu'ab* from Ka'b At-Tabi'i. The men of its *Isnad* (chains) are *Mawthuq* (trustworthy) (3740). See *Tahqiq Ash-Shu'ab*, published in India, no. 3465.

The Sanctity of Makkah

Makkah is known as the Sacred City (*Al-Balad Al-Haram*). It is clear from the words of Allâh's Messenger that Makkah has been sacred from the time Allâh created the heavens and the earth.

Abu Hurairah ﷺ narrated that when Allâh granted His Messenger ﷺ victory over Makkah, Allâh's Messenger ﷺ stood up before the people and praised and glorified Allâh, then he said:

"Allâh kept the Elephant away from Makkah, and He gave His Messenger and the believers authority over it. Fighting therein was never permitted to anyone before me; it was only permitted to me for a brief part of one day, and it will never be permitted for anyone after me. Its game should not be chased, its thorny bushes should not be uprooted and things that are dropped therein should not be picked up except by one who makes a public announcement. One whose relative is murdered has the option either to accept compensation for it, or to retaliate."

Al-'Abbas ﷺ said: "Except *Al-Idhkhir*,[3] O Messenger of Allâh, for we use it in our graves and in our homes." He said: "Except *Al-Idhkhir*." (Agreed upon)[4]

---

[3] *Al-Idhkhir*: a fragrant plant like palm fibres or raffia.
[4] *Al-Bukhari* (2434), *Muslim* (1345).

The Boundaries of the *Haram* (Sanctuary)

The first one to set up boundaries for the *Haram* was Ibrahim Al-Khalil ﷺ.

Ibrahim ﷺ set up boundary markers for the *Haram*, as shown by Jibril ﷺ, which were not moved until during the year of the Conquest, Allâh's Messenger ﷺ sent Tamim bin Asad Al-Khuza'i to renew them. Then they were not moved until the time of 'Umar bin Al-Khattab ﷺ, when he sent four men from Quraish to renew them.[5]

When Allâh made the Sacred House holy, He also made it a place of safety and security even for the birds and trees. And He decreed that the reward for deeds done there would be greater than the reward for deeds done elsewhere. The *Haram* is a circle around Makkah Al-Mukarramah, some parts of which are closer than others. Signs have been set upon the main roads leading into Makkah, which are as follows:

1- On the Jeddah road from the west: Ash-Shumaysi (Al-Hudaibiyah), which is 22 km away.

2- From the south: Ida'at Libn,[6] on the Yemen road coming from Tihamah, which is 12 km away.

---

[5] Reported by Al-Azraqi in *Akhbar Makkah* (2/129).
[6] *Ida'ah* means land, *Libn* is the name of a mountain.

3- From the east: the edge of Wadi 'Uranah Al-Gharbiyah, which is 15 km away.

4- From the northeast: Al-Ji'ranah road, near the village of Shara'i' Al-Mujahidin, which is 16 km away.

5- From the north: the boundary of At-Tan'im, which is seven km away

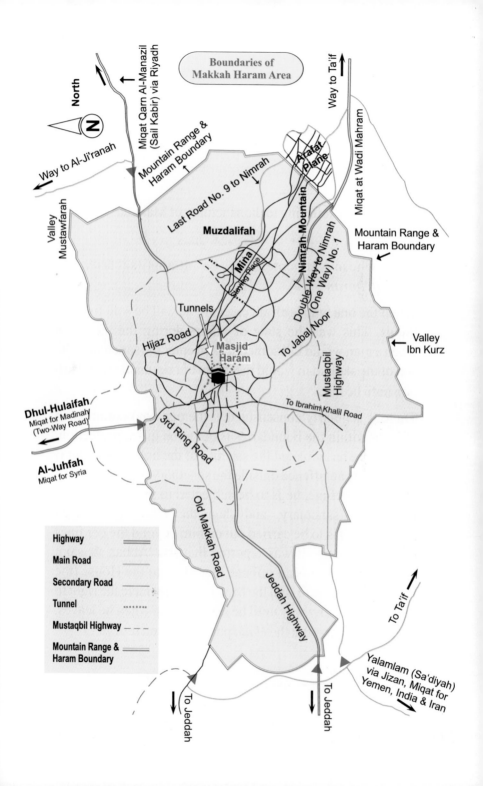

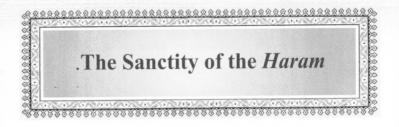

The Sanctity of the *Haram*

Allâh says referring to the sanctuary of Makkah:

﴿ وَمَن دَخَلَهُ كَانَ ءَامِنًا ﴾ [آل عمران:٩٧]

"...whosoever enters it, he attains security."
[*Aal 'Imran* 3:97]

When the one who is afraid enters it, he will be safe from all things. This was the state of affairs during the *Jahiliyah* when a man would kill someone then enter the sanctuary; the son of the slain man would meet him but be unable to disturb him until he left.[7]

There is scholarly consensus that the one who commits an offence within the boundaries is not to be given protection, because he has violated the sanctity of the holy place. But if he commits an offence outside the sanctuary then flees to the *Haram* for refuge, he is to be subjected to pressure until he leaves the sanctuary, and then the *Hadd* (prescribed punishment) is to be carried out on him beyond the confines of the sanctuary. It was reported that Ibn 'Abbas ﷺ said: "Whoever commits an offence then flees to the House (the Ka'bah) will be safe, and the Muslims do not have the right to punish him in any way until he leaves. Then when he leaves, they should carry out the *Hadd* punishment on him."[8]

---

[7] *Tafsir Ibn Kathir.*
[8] *Muthir Al-Gharam As-Sakin* by Ibn Al-Jawzi.

The Names of Makkah

The Holy City has many names, approximately fifty.[9] Allâh called Makkah by five names: Makkah, Bakkah, Al-Balad, Al-Qaryah and Ummul-Qura. He used the name Makkah in the Verse:

﴿ وَهُوَ ٱلَّذِى كَفَّ أَيْدِيَهُمْ عَنكُمْ وَأَيْدِيَكُمْ عَنْهُم بِبَطْنِ مَكَّةَ ﴾

[الفتح: ٢٤]

"And He it is Who has withheld their hands from you and your hands from them in the midst of Makkah" [Al-Fath 48:24]

Allâh mentioned the name Bakkah in the Verse:

﴿ إِنَّ أَوَّلَ بَيْتٍ وُضِعَ لِلنَّاسِ لَلَّذِى بِبَكَّةَ مُبَارَكًا وَهُدًى لِّلْعَٰلَمِينَ ﴾

[آل عمران: ٩٦]

"Verily, the first House (of worship) appointed for mankind was that at Bakkah (Makkah), full of blessing, and a guidance for Al-'Aalamin (mankind and jinn)" [Aal 'Imran 3:96]

He called it Al-Balad (the city), meaning Makkah, in the Verse:"

﴿ لَآ أُقْسِمُ بِهَٰذَا ٱلْبَلَدِ ﴾ [البلد:١]

I swear by this city (Makkah)." [Al-Balad 90:1]

---

[9] See *Shifa'ul-Gharam* (1/48-53); *Mu'jamul-Buldan* (5/181-183).

In Arabic the word *Balad* means the main city.

He called it Al-Qaryah (the township) in the Verse:

[النحل: ١١٢].

"And Allâh puts forward the example of a township (Makkah), that dwelt secure and well-content." [*An-Nahl* 16:112]

A *Qaryah* is a place in which a great number of people live together. It is a name derived from a verb which means to collect or gather, as in the phrase *Qaraytul-Ma' fil-Hawd* (I gathered the water in the cistern). And He called it Ummul-Qura (the Mother of Towns) in the Verse:

﴿ وَلِتُنذِرَ أُمَّ ٱلْقُرَىٰ ﴾ [الأنعام: ٩٢]

"…so that you may warn the Mother of Towns (i.e., Makkah)…" [*Al-An'am* 6:92], meaning Makkah.

Makkah also has other names such as: An-Nassasah, Al-Hatimah, Al-Haram, Salah, Al-Basah, Mu'adh, Ar-Ra's, Al-Balad Al-Amin, Kawtha and many others.

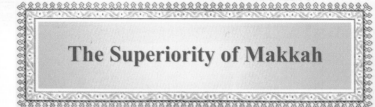

The Superiority of Makkah

There are many *Ahadith* which describe the virtues of Makkah and its high status before Allâh and His Messenger ﷺ. One of these *Ahadith* is the *Hadith* of 'Abdullah bin 'Adi bin Al-Hamra', who said that he heard Allâh's Messenger ﷺ saying in Makkah, whilst he was on his camel in Al-Hazwarah[10]:

> "By Allâh, you are the best land of Allâh, the most beloved land of Allâh to Allâh. Had I not been driven out of you, I would not have left you."[11]

This – the *Hadith* of Ibn Al-Hamra' – is the most authentic of the *Ahadith* narrated on this topic. It is the evidence cited by those who say that Makkah is superior to other places.

To explain the superiority of Makkah, it is sufficient to note that the reward for prayer in Al-Masjid Al-Haram is multiplied many times. It was reported that Jabir bin 'Abdullah ﷺ narrated that Allâh's Messenger ﷺ said:

> "A prayer in this mosque of mine is better than one thousand prayers anywhere else, except for Al-Masjid

---

[10] Al-Hazwarah was a market in Makkah in the courtyard of Umm Hani, which was incorporated into Al-Masjid Al-Haram. For more details on this topic see *Zadul-Ma'ad* by Ibn Al-Qaiyim (2/420-425), published by Matba'ah Ansar As-Sunnah Al-Muhammadiyah in Cairo.

[11]The source of this *Hadith* has been described above, in the section on the importance of Makkah.

Al-Haram. A prayer in Al-Masjid Al-Haram is better than one hundred thousand prayers (anywhere else)."[12]

If we calculate the superiority of one prayer in Al-Masjid Al-Haram according to the *Hadith* which says that one prayer there is one hundred thousand times better than prayer elsewhere, then one prayer in Al-Masjid Al-Haram is equivalent to the five daily prayers offered over a period of fifty-five years, six months and twenty days, and the five prayers offered over a single twenty-four hour period are equivalent to the five daily prayers offered over a period of two hundred and seventy-seven years, nine months and ten days.

---

[12] Ahmad (3/342, 397).

The *Hadith* which says that the reward for prayer is multiplied, also indicates that the reward for every good deed is multiplied one hundred thousand times. Al-Muhibb At-Tabari said: "The *Ahadith* quoted above which say that the reward for prayer and fasting is multiplied, also apply by analogy to the multiplication of the reward for all good deeds."[13] Al-Hasan Al-Basri said: "Fasting for one day in Makkah is equivalent to fasting one hundred thousand days, and giving one dirham in charity is like giving one hundred thousand; every good deed is equivalent to one hundred thousand."[14]

Two conditions must be met in order for the reward to be multiplied by one hundred thousand: the act must be done sincerely for the sake of Allâh alone, and it must be done following the *Sunnah* of His Messenger ﷺ.

The Muslim must avoid committing sin in Makkah, for just as the reward for good deeds is multiplied, so too the burden of bad deeds is also multiplied. Mujahid said: "The burden of bad deeds is multiplied in Makkah just as the reward for good deeds is multiplied."[15]

Imam Ahmad bin Hanbal was asked: "Is more than one *Sayi'ah* recorded for a bad deed?" He said: "No, except in Makkah, because of the sanctity of the land." Ibn Mas'ud ﷺ likewise said: "If a man resolves at the Ka'bah to kill a believer who is far away in 'Aden, Allâh will cause him to taste a painful torment in this world."[16]

---

[13] *Mana'ihul-Karam* (1/234). See also *Manasik An-Nawawi* (p. 407); *Al-Qira* by Al-Muhibb At-Tabari (p. 658).

[14] *Fada'il Makkah* by Al-Hasan Al-Basri (p. 21).

[15] *Muthir Al-Gharam* (P. 234).

[16] *Ahmad* (1/227, 310).

Living in Makkah

Living in Makkah is *Mustahab* (desirable) because of the multiplied reward for good deeds and acts of worship. Uncountable numbers of those who are examples to be followed, among the earlier and later generations of the *Ummah*, have lived there. One of the greatest signs that it is *Mustahab* to live there is the fact that the Prophet ﷺ wished to live there, and Bilal ؓ expressed in his poetry the wish to return to Makkah.[17]

One of the most eloquent things that have been said regarding emigration to Makkah and living there is what was said by Az-Zamakhshari in *Al-Kashshaf*: "We have tried and people before us have tried, and we have not found any place that is more conducive to subduing the self, resisting desires, focusing the mind, concentrating one's resolve, making one content with one's lot, repelling the *Shaytan* (Satan), keeping away from temptation and better for one's religious commitment in general, than living in the sanctuary of Allâh, close to the House of Allâh. To Allâh is the praise for having made that easy, blessing us with patience and inspiring us with gratitude."[18]

---

[17] See *Al-Bukhari* (3926).
[18] *Al-Kashshaf* (3/464).

Description of the Holy Ka'bah and the History of its Construction and Maintenance

Allâh says:

﴿ ۞ جَعَلَ ٱللَّهُ ٱلۡكَعۡبَةَ ٱلۡبَيۡتَ ٱلۡحَرَامَ قِيَٰمٗا لِّلنَّاسِ ﴾ [المائدة:٩٧]

"Allâh has made the Ka'bah, the Sacred House, an asylum of security and benefits (e.g., *Hajj* and *'Umrah*) for mankind." [*Al-Ma'idah* 5:97]

The Ka'bah is the Sacred House of Allâh in the middle of the Mosque. The reason why it is called the Ka'bah is that which was reported by Al-Azraqi from Abu Nujaih, who said: it is called the Ka'bah because it is cubiform (*Muka'ab*), i.e., in the shape of a cube (*Ka'b*). It is so called because it is square (*Murabba'*). 'Ikrimah and Mujahid said likewise.

And it was said that it is called Ka'bah because of its elevation above ground level.

It is also called *Al- Bait Al- 'Atiq*

(the Emancipated House) because Allâh freed it (*A'taqahu*) from coming under the control of tyrants, as 'Abdullah bin Az-Zubair ﷺ narrated that the Prophet ﷺ said:

> "It is called *Al-Bait Al-'Atiq* (the Ancient House) because Allâh freed it (*A'taqahu*) from coming under the control of tyrants, and no tyrant ever prevailed over it."[19]

The Construction of the Ka'bah

The Ka'bah has been built more than once; the most famous occasions on which it was rebuilt are five:

The first time it was built by the angels; the second time it was rebuilt by Adam ﷺ. The third time it was rebuilt by

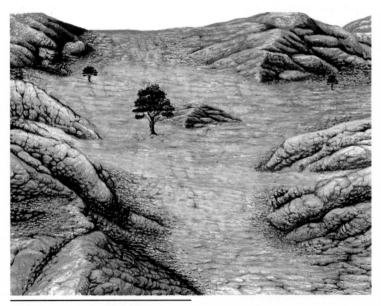

---

[19] *At-Tirmidhi* (3170).

Ibrahim ﷺ. The fourth time it was rebuilt by Quraish during the *Jahiliyah*, and this was witnessed by the Prophet ﷺ when he was twenty-five years old. The fifth time it was rebuilt by Ibn Az-Zubair ﷺ.

How Ibrahim ﷺ and Isma'il ﷺ built the Ka'bah

When Isma'il ﷺ was born to Hajrah (may peace be upon her), Sarah became intensely jealous of her and asked Ibrahim ﷺ to take her away from her. Allâh revealed to Ibrahim ﷺ that he should take Hajrah and her son to Makkah, so Ibrahim ﷺ took her and her child, and traveled until he left them in the place where Makkah stands today.

After leaving Hajrah and her son there, he used to visit them and keep a check on them. On one of his visits he found Isma'il ﷺ sharpening an arrow beneath a tree, close to

Zamzam. When Isma'il saw him, he stood up, and they greeted one another as fathers and sons do, then Ibrahim said, "O Isma'il, Allâh has commanded me to do something." Isma'il عليه السلام said, "Do what your Lord has commanded you to do." Ibrahim عليه السلام said, "Will you help me?" He said, "I will help you." He said, "Allâh has commanded me to build a house here," – and he pointed to a small rise in the land that was higher than the land around it. So, they laid the foundations of the House, then Isma'il عليه السلام started to bring the stones and Ibrahim عليه السلام started to build. Then when the structure got higher, he brought this stone (*Al-Maqam*) and put it down for him. Ibrahim عليه السلام stood on the stone and carried on the building work with Isma'il عليه السلام handing the stones up to him, and they were both saying while they were going around the House:

﴿ رَبَّنَا تَقَبَّلْ مِنَّا إِنَّكَ أَنتَ ٱلسَّمِيعُ ٱلْعَلِيمُ ﴾ [البقرة:١٢٧]

"Our Lord! Accept (this service) from us. Verily, You are the All-Hearer, the All-Knower." [*Al-Baqarah* 2:127]

How Quraish rebuilt the Ka'bah

Shortly before the Prophet's mission began, the Ka'bah was a structure of stones, built without mortar, the height of which was a little greater than the height of a man. Some people had come and stolen the treasure of the Ka'bah, which was in a well inside the building. Quraish wanted to rebuild it and put a roof on it. A ship belonging to a Roman merchant had been wrecked off the coast of Jeddah and had been smashed to pieces, so they took its wood and prepared it to make a roof. But then the people were scared to knock the Ka'bah down. Then Al-Walid bin Al-Mughirah started to knock it down, and when nothing happened to him, the people joined him in knocking it down.

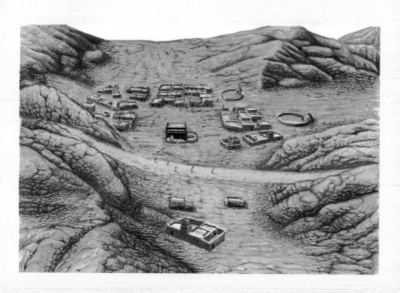

The Prophet ﷺ put the Black Stone in place

Then the tribes of Quraish started to gather stones for building, each tribe collecting stones by itself. They started to build, until they got to the place where the Black Stone was to be put, then they disputed concerning it, as each tribe wanted to lift the Stone and put it into the place on its own. They were about to resort to 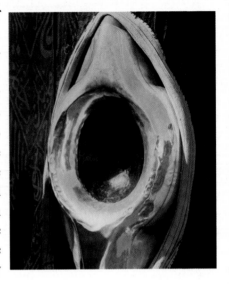 violence and were preparing to fight, they stayed like that for four or five days. Then they met in the mosque and consulted one another, asking one another to be fair.

Some narrators claim that Abu Umaiyah bin Al-Mughirah bin 'Abdullah bin 'Umar bin Makhzum, who at that time was the most senior of them all, said: "O Quraish, come to an agreement concerning that over which you are disputing. Let the first man who enters through the gate of this mosque decide the matter for you."

The first man to come through the gate was Allâh's Messenger ﷺ. When they saw him, they said: "This is *Al-Amin* (the trustworthy one), we agree to accept Muhammad's decision." When he came to them and they told him what was happening, he said: "Bring me a cloak." So, they

brought it, then he picked up the Stone with his own hands and placed it on the cloak. Then he said: "Let each tribe take an edge of the cloak, and all of you lift it up together." So, they did that until they brought it to its place, then he himself put it in its place, and construction continued above that point.[20]

How Ibn Az-Zubair 🙰 rebuilt the Ka'bah

When 'Abdullah bin Az-Zubair 🙰 stayed behind and did not offer the pledge of allegiance (Bai'ah) to Yazid bin Mu'awiyah, and he became scared of them, he went to Makkah to seek sanctuary in the *Haram*. He gathered his supporters and began to criticize Yazid and condemn Banu Umaiyah.

---

[20] *Seerat Ibn Hisham* (1/233, 234).

News of that reached Yazid, so he decided to send an army to bring 'Abdullah to him in chains. Whilst he was preparing the army, news reached Yazid about the people of Al-Madinah and what they had done to his governor and the members of Banu Umaiyah who were with him in Al-Madinah, and how they had expelled them from the city, except for those who were descended from 'Uthman bin 'Affan ﷺ. Yazid sent an army to fight the people of Al-Madinah, and when they had defeated them and entered the city, the army moved on to Makkah under the leadership of Al-Husain bin Numair. They fought Ibn Az-Zubair ﷺ for a few days. Ibn Az-Zubair gathered his companions and barricaded himself with them in Al-Masjid Al-Haram and around the Ka'bah, with the result that there were many tents around the Ka'bah. One of the tents caught fire, and there was a strong wind that day.

The Ka'bah at that time was as it had been built by Quraish, with alternate layers of teak and stones from bottom to top, covered with the *Kiswah* (fabric cover). The wind carried a flame that set fire to the cover of the Ka'bah, and the teak parts of the structure burned. It caught fire on a Saturday, the third night of Rabi'ul-Awwal 64 AH. The walls of the Ka'bah were thus weakened and it started to collapse from top to bottom; if a bird landed on it, stones would start to fly everywhere.

The Makkans and the Syrians[21] all panicked. Al-Husain bin Numair was besieging Ibn Az-Zubair. Ibn Zubair ﷺ sent some of the men of Makkah, from Quraish and other tribes,

---

[21] i.e., the army that had come from Syria.

to tell Husain that Yazid to whom Ibn Az-Zubair 🙏 had refused to give allegiance, had died – he had died twenty-seven days after the fire in the Ka'bah – (and to ask:) "So, why are we fighting? Go back to Syria and wait and see what will happen with regard to the new caliph," – meaning Mu'awiyah bin Yazid, and whether the people would agree to him becoming caliph. They kept trying to persuade him until he gave in and went back to Syria.

When the army of Husain bin Numair left Makkah on the fifth day of Rabi'ul-Akhir 64 AH, Ibn Az-Zubair 🙏 called the leaders and nobles of the people and consulted with them about knocking the Ka'bah down. Only a few of them said that he should knock it down; most of them disagreed and said that he should not do that. The one who most strongly opposed was 'Abdullah bin 'Abbas 🙏 who said to him: "Leave it in the state that Allâh's Messenger ﷺ approved of, for I am afraid that there may come after you people who will knock it down, and they will keep knocking it down and rebuilding it until people will lose respect for it. Rather you should repair it."

Ibn Az-Zubair 🙏 said: "By Allâh, none of you would agree to simply patch up the house of his mother and father, so how can I patch up the House of Allâh when I can see that it is collapsing from top to bottom, and even when the birds land on it, stones fly out in all directions?"

Ibn Az-Zubair 🙏 spent several days consulting with them, and then they agreed to knock it down. He wanted to be the one to rebuild it according to what Allâh's Messenger ﷺ had said about the foundations of Isma'il ﷺ. In *As-Sahihain* it is

narrated from 'Aishah ﷺ that the Prophet ﷺ said to her:

> "Do you not see that when your people (i.e., Quraish) rebuilt the Ka'bah, they did not build fully on the foundations of Ibrahim?" She said: "O Messenger of Allâh, why do you not restore it on the foundations of Ibrahim?" Allâh's Messenger ﷺ said: "Were it not that your people are still so close to the time of *Kufr* (i.e., too new in Islam), I would have done that."

Ibn 'Umar ﷺ said:

> "I never saw Allâh's Messenger ﷺ fail to acknowledge the two corners which face the Hijr because the Ka'bah was not built on all the foundations of Ibrahim."[22]

'Aishah ﷺ said:

> "I asked him: 'Why is its door high up?' He said: 'Your

---

[22] *Al-Bukhari* (1583).

people did that so that they could admit whomever they wished and keep out whomever they wished."[23]

According to another *Hadith,* the Prophet ﷺ said:

"Were it not that your people are still so close to the time of *Kufr,* I would have knocked the Ka'bah down and rebuilt it with two doors, a door through which the people could enter and a door through which they could exit."

So, Ibn Az-Zubair did that.[24] He knocked down the Ka'bah and rebuilt it on the foundations of Ibrahim ﷺ, as Quraish had fallen short in that regard.[25] He incorporated the *Hijr* into the House, and gave it two doors, one on the east and one on the west.[26]

When Ibn Az-Zubair ﷺ had finished rebuilding the Ka'bah, he clothed it inside and out, from top to bottom, and covered it with *Qibati* (a kind of cloth). Then he said: "Whoever has sworn allegiance to me, let him go out and start *'Umrah* (lesser pilgrimage) from At-Tan'im; whoever is able to sacrifice a *Badanah* (a cow or camel), then let him do so; whoever is not able to sacrifice a *Badanah,* then let him offer a sheep. He set out walking and the people set out with him walking, until they did *'Umrah* from At-Tan'im, giving thanks to Allâh. There was never a day when more slaves were set free, more sacrifices were offered and more charity was given, than that day.

---

[23] *Al Bukhari* (1584*), Muslim* (3/273).

[24] *Akhbar Makkah* by Al-Azraqi, 1/100-219.

[25] It was said that they did not have sufficient *Halal* money.

[26] *Akhbar Makkah* by Al-Azraqi, 1/205.

Ibn Az-Zubair ﷺ sacrificed one hundred *Badanah*, and when he did *Tawaf* (circumambulation) around the Ka'bah, he touched all four corners, and said: "These two corners – the Syrian and western – were not touched because the House was not complete. The House remained as Ibn Az-Zubair ﷺ had built it, and when anyone did *Tawaf* around it, he would touch all four corners, entering the House through one door and exiting through the western door, with the doors at ground level, until Ibn Az-Zubair ﷺ was killed.

Then Al-Hajjaj entered Makkah and wrote to 'Abdul-Malik bin Marwan, telling him what Ibn Az-Zubair had added to the Ka'bah. 'Abdul-Malik bin Marwan wrote to him telling him to block up the western door which Ibn Az-Zubair had opened, to knock down the extension that Ibn Az-Zubair had built. So, Al-Hajjaj knocked down six cubits plus one hand span from the side of the *Hijr* and restored it to the way it had been before. Then the caliph came to know of the *Hadith* of 'Aishah ﷺ and he regretted what he had done, but he left it and did not add

anything. This story is reported in *Sahih Muslim.*[27]

During his reign, Caliph Al-Walid bin 'Abdul-Malik sent thirty-six thousand dinars (gold coins) to his governor in Makkah, and the door and downspout (*Mizab*) of the Ka'bah were covered with gold plates, as were the columns and interior corners. Al-Walid was the first person in Islam to adorn the House with gold.

The Incident of the Elephant

During the time of 'Abdul-Muttalib there happened a major event which was recorded for posterity in the Qur'ân. This was the incident of the Elephant. The Ethiopian Abrahah, who was ruling Yemen, had built a church, which he called Al-Qullais. He wanted to divert the pilgrimage of the Arabs from the Ka'bah to this church. The Arabs were angered by that, and a man from Kinanah came and desecrated the church. When Abrahah came to know of that, he became angry and swore to go to the House and destroy it. Then he ordered the Abyssinian army to get ready, and he set out, with the elephant.

When Abrahah reached Al-Mughammas,[28] he sent one of the Abyssinian men whose name was Al-Aswad bin Maqsud, as commander of a detachment of cavalry. He went to Makkah and brought back to Abrahah the wealth of the people of Tihamah, Quraish and others, among which were two hundred camels belonging to 'Abdul-Muttalib bin Hashim, who at that time was the leader of Quraish. Quraish, Kinanah, Hudhail and other tribes who were in the *Haram*,

---

[27] *Muslim* (1333).
[28] A place on the way to At-Ta'if.

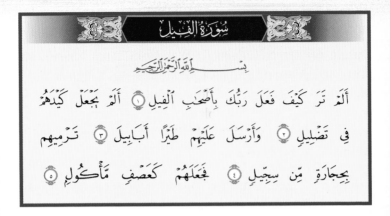

سُوۡرَةُ الفِيل

بِسۡمِ ٱللَّهِ ٱلرَّحۡمَٰنِ ٱلرَّحِيمِ

أَلَمۡ تَرَ كَيۡفَ فَعَلَ رَبُّكَ بِأَصۡحَٰبِ ٱلۡفِيلِ ۝ أَلَمۡ يَجۡعَلۡ كَيۡدَهُمۡ فِي تَضۡلِيلٍ ۝ وَأَرۡسَلَ عَلَيۡهِمۡ طَيۡرًا أَبَابِيلَ ۝ تَرۡمِيهِم بِحِجَارَةٍ مِّن سِجِّيلٍ ۝ فَجَعَلَهُمۡ كَعَصۡفٍ مَّأۡكُولٍۭ ۝

resolved to fight Abrahah, then they realized that they were unable to do so, so they gave up the idea.

Abrahah sent Hunatah Al-Himyari to Makkah with the instructions to ask about the leader of the people of that land and then deliver him the message from the king: "I have not come to wage war against you, for I have only come to destroy this House. If you do not fight me then I have no need to shed your blood." Abrahah then said to him: "If he does not want to wage war against me, then bring him to me."

When Hunatah reached Makkah, he asked about the leader of Quraish and he was told that the leader was 'Abdul-Muttalib bin Hashim. So, he came to him and told him what Abrahah had told him to say. 'Abdul-Muttalib said to him: "By Allâh, we do not want to wage war against him, and we are not able to do so. This is the Sacred House of Allâh, and the House of His close Friend Ibrahim. If He prevents him, then it is His House and His sanctuary, and if He lets him do it then we cannot ward him off." Hunatah said to him: "Come with me to Abrahah, for he has commanded me to bring you to him."

'Abdul-Muttalib was the most handsome and dignified of men, and when Abrahah saw him, he was filled with respect and admiration so much so that he thought that he should not make him sit beneath him, but he also did not want the Abyssinians see him sitting with him on his throne. So, Abrahah came down from his throne and sat on his carpet, and seated 'Abdul-Muttalib beside him. Then he told his interpreter to ask him: "What do you need?" So, the interpreter asked him. 'Abdul-Muttalib said: "I need my wealth back, the two hundred camels which belong to me and were taken by you." When he said that, Abrahah said to his interpreter to tell him: "I was impressed with you when I saw you, but when you spoke to me, I lost respect for you, because you spoke to me about the two hundred camels that belong to you, but you said nothing about the House which is part of your religion and the religion of your forefathers, which I have come to destroy. Why did you not mention it?" 'Abdul-Muttalib said: "I am the owner of the camels, and the House has an Owner Who will protect it." Abrahah said: "No one can prevent me from reaching it." 'Abdul-Muttalib said: "You will see."

Abrahah returned 'Abdul-Muttalib's camels to him, and 'Abdul-Muttalib went back to Quraish and told them to leave Makkah and hide on the mountaintops, fearing that they would be harshly treated by the invading army.

Then 'Abdul-Muttalib stood up and took hold of the handle on the door of the Ka'bah, and a group from Quraish stood with him, praying to Allâh and seeking His help against Abrahah and his troops. 'Abdul-Muttalib said, holding on to the handle of the door of the Ka'bah:

"O Allâh, just as Your slave would protect his property, so protect Your property. Do not let their cross and their power defeat Your Power tomorrow."

When Abrahah was ready to enter Makkah, he prepared his elephant, whose name was Mahmud, and mobilized his troops. He had decided to destroy the House then return to Yemen. When they tried to make the elephant move in the direction of Makkah, it sat down. They beat it to make it stand up, but it refused. Then they told it to go in the direction of Yemen and it stood up and started running. When they told it to go in the direction of Syria, and to the east, it did likewise, but when they again tried to make it move in the direction of Makkah, it sat down again.

Then Allâh sent against them birds from the sea, each of which was carrying three stones, one in its beak and two in its talons. The stones were like chickpeas and lentils, and no one was hit with them but he died. They fled, falling about and dying all over the place. Abrahah was also struck on his

body, and they took him back, with his fingertips dropping off one by one, until they brought him to San'a', and by that time he was as helpless as an infant bird, and there he died. The incident of the Elephant had a great effect on Quraish and on their standing among the Arab tribes. When Allâh drove the Abyssinians away from Makkah and wreaked His vengeance upon them, the Arabs venerated Quraish and called them the 'people of Allâh', saying that Allâh had fought on their behalf and dealt with their enemy for them.

This event also raised the status of 'Abdul-Muttalib and made him famous and well respected among all the Arabs, for he had handled the matter well and protected his people from great danger.

The Destruction of the Ka'bah at the End of Time

There are *Ahadith* of the Prophet ﷺ that confirm that the Ka'bah will be destroyed at the end of time. It was reported that Abu Hurairah ؓ narrated that Allâh's Messenger ﷺ said:

"The Ka'bah will be destroyed by Dhus-Suwaiqatain (a man with thin legs) from Abyssinia."[29]

It was reported that 'Ali ؓ narrated that the Prophet ﷺ said:

"Do a lot of *Tawaf* around this House, as much as you can before you are prevented from doing so. It is as if I can see him, with a small head and small ears, destroying it with his shovel."[30]

It was narrated by Ibn 'Abbas ؓ that Allâh's Messenger ﷺ

---

[29] *Al-Bukhari* (1591).
[30] *Akhbar Makkah* by Al-Fakihi (313).

يُخَرِّبُ الكَعبَة
ذُو السُّوَيقَتَينِ مِنَ الحَبَشَة

said:

> "It is as if I can see him, black and bow-legged, knocking it down stone by stone."

It was reported from Sa'eed bin Sam'an that he heard Abu Hurairah ﴿ telling Abu Qatadah that Allâh's Messenger ﷺ said:

> "Allegiance will be sworn to a man between the *Rukn* and the *Maqam*, and no one will violate the sanctity of this House except its own people. When they violate it, do not ask about the destruction of the Arabs. Then the Abyssinians will come and destroy it in such a way that it will never be rebuilt, and they are the ones who will extract its treasure."[31]

This *Hadith* does not contradict the *Hadith* of 'Aishah ﴿, according to which the Prophet ﷺ said:

> "An army will attack the Ka'bah and when they reach an area of plain ground, the earth will swallow them up, the first and the last of them."[32]

---

[31] *Ahmad* (2/291); *Al-Hakim* (4/452); *Majma'uz-Zawa'id* (3/298).
[32] *Al-Bukhari* (2118).

Ibn Hajar said in his book *Fath Al-Bari, Bab Hadam Al-Ka'bah* (chapter on the destruction of the Ka'bah): "This indicates that there will be attacks against the Ka'bah, one time Allâh will destroy them before they reach it and another time He will permit them to reach it. The apparent meaning is that the attack of those who will destroy it will happen after the first attack."[33]

No one should say: "Allâh kept the Elephant from reaching Makkah and did not allow its owners to destroy the Ka'bah, and it was not a *Qiblah* at that time, so how can the Abyssinians gain power over it after it has become the *Qiblah* of the Muslims?" – because the report is to be understood as meaning that this will happen at the end of time, shortly before the Hour begins, when there will be no one left on earth who will say "Allâh, Allâh," as it was proven in *Sahih Muslim*:

"The Hour will not begin until it is no longer said on earth: 'Allâh, Allâh.'"[34]

Hence it says in the *Hadith* of Sa'eed bin Sam'an: "…it will never be rebuilt."

---

[33] *Fath Al-Bari, Kitabul-Hajj, Bab Hadam Al-Ka'bah.*
[34] *Muslim* (148).

Custodianship of the Ka'bah

'Umar bin Al-Khattab ﷺ used to say to Quraish:

"The guardians of this House before you were Tasm, but they lost respect for it and violated its sanctity, so Allâh destroyed them. Then guardianship passed to Jurhum, but they lost respect for it and violated its sanctity, so Allâh destroyed them. So, do not lose respect for it, and honor its sanctity."[35]

The authors of *Seerah* said: When Jurhum lost respect for it, Allâh scattered them and guardianship passed to Khuza'ah; then after Khuza'ah, Qusai bin Kilab became the custodian of the Ka'bah and in charge of Makkah. Then custodianship was given to his son 'Abdud-Dar, and he also became the custodian of the place of meeting and the banner of Quraish. It was called a place of meeting because it was a place where people gathered to decide their affairs and consult with one another. 'Abd Manaf was given the responsibility of providing water and help to the pilgrims. Then 'Abdud-Dar passed the role of gatekeeper to his son 'Uthman, and the position was handed down from father to son until it reached 'Uthman bin Talhah.

'Uthman said: "We used to open the Ka'bah on Mondays and Thursdays. Allâh's Messenger ﷺ came one day wanting to enter with the people, and I annoyed him but he was patient

---

[35] Reported by Al-Baihaqi in *Ad-Dala'il* (2/49, 50), and by 'Abdur-Razzaq (9107).

with me. Then he said, 'O 'Uthman, perhaps one day you will see this key in my hand and I will give it to whomever I wish.' I said, 'That will be when Quraish is doomed and humiliated!' He said, 'On the contrary, they will be honored.' He went inside the Ka'bah, and I began to think about what he had said. I thought that things would turn out as he said, and I wanted to become Muslim, but my people rebuked me and told me off. When Allâh's Messenger ﷺ entered Makkah in the year when he made up *'Umrah* after having been turned back the previous year, Allâh changed my heart and caused me to enter Islam, but I did not have the resolve to go to him until he had gone back to Al-Madinah. Then I decided to go to him, so I left at night, and I met Khalid bin Al-Walid, so we went on together. Then we met 'Amr bin Al-'Aas, and we went on together until we reached Al-Madinah, where we swore our allegiance to the Prophet ﷺ. I stayed with him until I went out with him on the campaign that resulted in the conquest of Makkah. When he entered Makkah he said:

'O 'Uthman, bring the key.'

I brought it to him and he took it from me, then he gave it back to me and said:

'Take it, O Banu Talhah, for ever and ever. No one will take it from you except one who is a wrongdoer.'"

Ibn 'Abbas ﷺ narrated that when Allâh's Messenger ﷺ asked 'Uthman for the key and he was about to give it to him, Al-'Abbas said to him, "May my mother and father be sacrificed for you, give it to me along with the right to provide water for the pilgrims." 'Uthman held on to the key, fearing that the Prophet ﷺ would give it to Al-'Abbas bin

'Abdul-Muttalib. The Prophet ﷺ said, "Give me the key."
Al-'Abbas repeated what he had said, and 'Uthman held on
to the key. The Prophet ﷺ said, "Give me the key if you
believe in Allâh and the Last Day." He said, "Here it is, O
Messenger of Allâh, as a trust for the sake of Allâh." He
took the key and opened the door of the House, and then
Jibril brought the revelation to him:

﴿ ٨ إِنَّ ٱللَّهَ يَأْمُرُكُمْ أَن تُؤَدُّواْ ٱلْأَمَٰنَٰتِ إِلَىٰٓ أَهْلِهَا ﴾ [النساء:٥٨].

"Verily, Allâh commands that you should render back
the trusts to those to whom they are due' [An-Nisa'
4:58]

So 'Uthman continued to take care of the House until he died,
then the key passed to Shaibah bin 'Uthman bin Abi Talhah,
who was his paternal cousin, and the custodianship of the
Ka'bah remained in the hands of the descendants of Shaibah,
may Allâh be pleased with them.[36]

---

[36] *Mathir Al-Gharam As-Sakin, Bab Sidanat Al-Ka'bah.*

The Cover of the Ka'bah

This history of the cover of the Ka'bah is inseparable from the history of the Ka'bah itself. The level of concern with the cover of the Ka'bah is a reflection of the Muslims' concern with the Ka'bah and its sanctity and honor, and shows what a high status it holds in their hearts.

The Cover before Islam

Muhammad bin Ishaq said: I have heard from more than one scholars that the first one who covered the Ka'bah completely was Tubba' – who is As'ad Al-Himyari – who was shown in a dream that he should cover it, so he covered it with leather. Then he was shown that he should cover it with red-striped Yemeni cloth.

After Tubba', it was covered by many people during the *Jahiliyah*. That was regarded as a religious duty. Anybody who wanted to cover the Ka'bah was allowed to do so whenever he wanted, with any kind of fabric. So, the Ka'bah was covered with different kinds of covers, including thick cloth, thin cloth from the city of Ma'afir, fine cloth and cloth interwoven with gold thread.

The covers would be placed one on top of the other, until they became too heavy or wore out, then they would be removed and shared out or buried.

During the *Jahiliyah*, Quraish used to co-operate in covering

the Ka'bah. They would impose this duty upon the tribes as much as they could, from the time of Qusai bin Kilab until there came Abu Rabi'ah bin Al-Mughirah bin 'Abdullah bin 'Umar bin Makhzum. He used to travel to Yemen for the purpose of trade, and he had become rich. He said to Quraish: "I will cover the Ka'bah by myself one year, and all of Quraish will do it one year." So, he continued to do that

until he died; he would bring high quality striped cloth from Yemen and cover the Ka'bah with it. Quraish called him *Al-'Adl* (the equal or counterpart) because what he would do was equal to what all of Quraish did. So, they called him *Al-'Adl* and they called his sons *Banu Al-'Adl*.[37]

The first Arab woman to cover the Ka'bah with silk and brocade was Nubailah bint Jinab, the mother of Al-'Abbas bin 'Abdul-Muttalib.

The Covering of the Ka'bah in Islamic Times

Allâh's Messenger ﷺ and his *Sahabah* (Companions) did not cover the Ka'bah before the conquest of Makkah, because the *Kuffar* (disbelievers) did not let them do that. When Makkah was conquered, Allâh's Messenger ﷺ did not change the cover of the Ka'bah until it was burned by a woman who wanted to perfume it with incense. Then he covered it with Yemeni cloth, and Abu Bakr, 'Umar and 'Uthman ﷺ covered it with *Qibati* (thin white cloth from Egypt).

It was reported that Mu'awiyah bin Abi Sufyan used to cover the Ka'bah twice a year, with brocade on the day of *'Ashura'*, and with *Qibati* at the end of Ramadan. Then Yazid bin Mu'awiyah, Ibn Az-Zubair and 'Abdul-Malik bin Marwan covered it with brocade. The Ka'bah used to be covered twice every year, once with brocade and once with *Qibati*.

It was covered with brocade on the day of *At-Tarwiyah* (the eighth of Dhul-Hijjah), when the upper part of the cover would be hung. The lower part of the cover, which was also made of brocade, would be hung on the day of *'Ashura'*, after

---

[37] *Akhbar Makkah* by Al-Azraqi, 1/249.

the pilgrims had left, so that they would not damage it. The brocade cover would remain until the twenty-seventh day of Ramadan, when it would be covered with *Qibati* for *'Eidul-Fitr*.

At the time of Al-Ma'mun, the Ka'bah would be covered with three different covers: with red brocade on the day of *At-Tarwiyah*, with *Qibati* on the day when the new moon of Rajab was sighted, and with white brocade on the twenty-seventh day of Ramadan.

When Al-Ma'mun found out that the white brocade was being damaged during the days of *Hajj*, he had a fourth white cover made on the day of *At-Tarwiyah*. Then An-Nasir Al-'Abbasi covered it with green cloth, then with a black cloth. From that day it has always been covered with a black cloth.

The first of the kings to cover the Ka'bah after the end of the 'Abbasid period was Al-Muzaffar, the king of Yemen, in 659 AH. He continued to cover it for a number of years, along with the kings of Egypt. The first Egyptian ruler who strove to cover the Ka'bah after the 'Abbasids, was the King Az-Zahir Baibars Al-Bunduqdari, in 661 AH.

In 751 AH, the righteous king Isma'il bin Al-Malik An-Nasir Muhammad bin Qalawun, the king of Egypt, set up a *Waqf* (endowment) specifically to cover the Ka'bah with an outer black cover once a year and a green cover for the tomb of the Prophet ﷺ once every five years. But the Khedive Muhammad 'Ali dissolved this *Waqf* at beginning of the thirteenth century AH, after which the cover was made at the government's expense, and Turkey and whoever came into power after the Ottomans, had the exclusive right to provide

the inner cover of the Ka'bah.

In 810 AH the decorated cover was introduced which is placed on the outside of the Ka'bah and is called *Al-Burqa'*. That stopped during the years 816-818 AH, then it resumed in 819 AH and has continued until now.

The Cover during the Saudi Period

King 'Abdul-'Aziz bin 'Abdur-Rahman Aal Sa'ud (may Allâh have mercy on him) was concerned about taking care of the two Holy Places, and as a result of this concern, King Sa'ud bin 'Abdul-'Aziz (may Allâh have mercy on him) ordered that a special institution be set up to make the cover of the holy Ka'bah in Makkah Al-Mukarramah, and that everything needed for this work be provided.

Wanting to do the job properly and in a manner that befitted the holiness of the Ka'bah, His Majesty King Faisal bin

'Abdul-'Aziz Aal Sa'ud (may Allâh have mercy on him) issued orders in 1382 AH that a new factory be built to make the cover for the Ka'bah. The new factory was completed in 1397 AH in Umm Al-Jud, in Makkah Al-Mukarramah, equipped with modern machines for making the fabric, using automatic looms whilst also retaining the methods of crafts done by hand, because of their high artistic value. The factory is still keeping up with the latest developments whilst also preserving the ancient heritage of handicrafts to produce the cover of the Ka'bah in the finest way.[38]

---

[38] From the book *Masna' Kiswatul-Ka'bah Al-Musharrafah.*

Maqam Ibrahim (the Station of Ibrahim) and its Virtues

This is the stone on which Ibrahim ﷺ stood when he built the Ka'bah. Because that action was one of the most beloved actions to Allâh, He caused the trace of his footprints to remain as a reminder to the believers among his descendents and others, for them and for others. It was reported in a *Sahih* narration from Sa'eed bin Jubair ﷺ that the Prophet ﷺ said:

> "The stone is the Station of Ibrahim. Allâh made it soft and made it a mercy. Ibrahim would stand on it and Isma'il would hand the stones up to him."[39]

Anas ﷺ narrated that 'Umar bin Al-Khattab ﷺ said: My opinion was supported by my Lord in three cases. I said, "O Messenger of Allâh, why do we not take the Station of Ibrahim as a place of prayer?" Then this Verse was revealed:

﴿ وَٱتَّخِذُوا۟ مِن مَّقَامِ إِبْرَٰهِـۧمَ مُصَلًّى ﴾ [البقرة:١٢٥]

> "And take you (people) the *Maqam* (place) of Ibrahim (or the stone on which Ibrahim ﷺ stood while he was building the Ka'bah) as a place of prayer (for some of your prayers, e.g., two *Rak'at* after the *Tawaf* of the Ka'bah at Makkah)." [*Al-Baqarah* 2:125][40]

At-Tabari reported in his *Tafsir* via Sa'eed bin Abi 'Urubah that Qatadah said concerning this Verse: "They were

---

[39] *Muthir Al-Gharam* (p. 312).
[40] *Al-Bukhari* (4483).

commanded to offer prayer there, but they were not commanded to touch it. We have been told about it by those who have seen the marks of his heels and toes there, but the people kept touching it until they were worn away and vanished."

At the time of Ibrahim التَّلَامُ, the *Maqam* was attached to the Ka'bah, until it was moved back by 'Umar ﷺ to the place where it is now. This was reported by 'Abdur-Razzaq in his *Musannaf* with *Sahih Isnad* from 'Ata' and others, and also

from Mujahid. Al-Baihaqi reported a similar narration from 'Aishah 🌸 with a *Jaiyid Isnad* (good chain of narrators), which says:

> "During the time of the Prophet 🕌 and Abu Bakr, the *Maqam* was attached to the Ka'bah, then 'Umar moved it back."

Neither the *Sahabah* (Companions) nor those who came after them denounced 'Umar's actions, so there was consensus on this matter.

'Umar 🌸 thought that leaving it where it was, would make the space too crowded for *Tawaf* or for prayers, so he put it in a place that would make things easier for the people. He was guided in that, for he was the one who suggested that it should be taken as a place of prayer.[41]

---

[41] *Fath Al-Bari*, commentary on *Hadith* no. 4483.

Al-Hijr

Many *Ahadith* indicate that the Hijr is part of the House, and is included in the Verse:

﴿ وَلْيَطَّوَّفُوا بِالْبَيْتِ الْعَتِيقِ ﴾ [الحج:٢٩]

"…and circumambulate the Ancient House (the Ka'bah at Makkah)." [*Al-Hajj* 22:29]

Based on this, *Tawaf* must include going around the Hijr too; otherwise one's *Tawaf* is not valid.

Al-Hijr is the place where Ibrahim ﷺ left his wife Hajrah and son Isma'il when he brought them to Makkah and told Hajrah (may peace be upon her) to build a small hut there. Quraish included only part of Al-Hijr in the Ka'bah because the money they had prepared for building it ran short.

When 'Abdullah bin Az-Zubair ﷺ took over Makkah, he knocked down the Ka'bah and rebuilt it including the Hijr which Quraish had omitted from it. But Al-Hajjaj – after Ibn Az-Zubair ﷺ was killed – put it back as it was and built the wall on the foundations laid by Quraish, and this is how it has remained until the present day, with part of the Hijr included in the Ka'bah and part of it excluded. Among the evidence of that, is the *Hadith* of 'Aishah ﷺ that says:

"Were it not for the fact that your people are still so close to the time of *Shirk* or *Jahiliyah* – I would have knocked down the Ka'bah, brought the door down to

ground level, and made two doors for it, one on the east and one on the west, and I would have added six cubits of the Hijr to it, for Quraish reduced its area when they rebuilt the Ka'bah."[42]

Ibn 'Umar ﷺ said: "'Aishah heard this from Allâh's Messenger ﷺ, and I think that the only reason why Allâh's Messenger ﷺ did not touch the two corners which are opposite the Hijr is that the House was not built completely on the foundations laid by Ibrahim."[43]

Many of the scholars mentioned that Isma'il عليه السلام was buried in the Hijr beside the grave of his mother Hajrah (may peace be upon her). But the reports that have been narrated concerning that are all *Da'eef* (weak) and none of them are

---

[42] *Ahmad* (6/204).
[43] *Al-Bukhari* (1583).

Sahih. What indicates that they are not true is the fact that the senior *Sahabah* were present when Quraish rebuilt the Ka'bah and they witnessed the digging of the foundations at that time, but not one of them reported that they saw any trace of a grave. If that had been true, it would not have been permissible for us to step on the site of a grave, because the Prophet ﷺ forbade us to walk or sit on the graves.

According to many *Ahadith*, the one who enters the Hijr is like one who enters the Ka'bah. It was reported that 'Aishah ﷺ narrated:

> "I wanted to enter the House and pray inside. Allâh's Messenger ﷺ took me by the hand and led me inside the Hijr and said: 'If you want to go inside the House then pray here, for it is part of the House, but your people reduced its area when they rebuilt it.'"[44]

It was reported by 'Abdul-Hameed bin Jubair from his paternal aunt Safiyah bint Shaibah that 'Aishah ﷺ narrated to them her saying to the Prophet ﷺ: "O Messenger of Allâh, can I not enter the House?" He said: "Enter Al-Hijr, for it is part of the House."[45]

It was narrated in a *Sahih* report that Ibn 'Abbas ﷺ said: "Pray in the place where the Chosen prayed and drink the drink of the righteous." It was said to Ibn 'Abbas ﷺ: "What is the place where the Chosen prayed?" He said: "Beneath the downspout." He was asked, "What is the drink of the righteous?" He said: "The water of Zamzam."[46]

---

[44] *An-Nasa'i* (2912).
[45] *An-Nasa'i* (2911).
[46] Al-Azraqi (1/318).

This points to the virtue of praying in Al-Hijr. With regard to the report from Al-'Ata', according to which he said, "Whoever stands beneath the downspout of the Ka'bah and calls upon Allâh, his supplication will be answered and he will emerge free of sin as on the day his mother bore him,"[47] this is *Da'eef* (weak) and cannot be used to prove anything. This is a matter of the unseen and cannot be traced with a sound chain of narrators going back to the Prophet ﷺ or to any of the Companions.

---

[47] *Muthir Al-Gharam* (p. 269); he attributed it to Al-Azraqi and said its (*Isnad*) includes 'Uthman bin Saj.

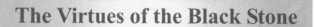

The Virtues of the Black Stone

There are many *Ahadith* that affirm the virtues of the Black Stone and urge us to touch it or kiss it when doing *Tawaf*. To know of its virtue, it is sufficient for us to know that it was touched by the hand of the Prophet ﷺ and kissed by his noble mouth.

As reported in *As-Sahihain* (the Two *Sahihs*, meaning *Sahih Al-Bukhari* and *Sahih Muslim*), 'Umar bin Al-Khattab ؓ kissed the Black Stone and said: "I know that you are only a stone and can neither do harm nor bring benefit. Had I not seen Allâh's Messenger ﷺ kissing you, I would not have kissed you."[48]

Ibn 'Abbas ؓ narrated that Allâh's Messenger ﷺ said:

> "The Black Stone came down from Paradise and it was whiter than milk, but the sins of the sons of Adam turned it black."[49]

Ibn 'Abbas ؓ narrated that Allâh's Messenger ﷺ said concerning the Stone:

> "By Allâh, Allâh will resurrect it on the Day of Resurrection with two eyes with which it will see and a tongue with which it will speak, and it will bear witness concerning those who touched it recognizing

---

[48] *Al-Bukhari* (1597) and *Muslim* (1270).
[49] *At-Tirmidhi* (877).

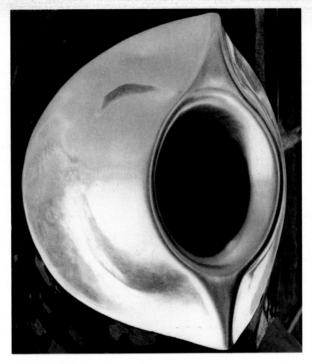

its virtue."[50]

Al-Musafi' bin Shaibah said that he heard 'Abdullah bin 'Amr bin Al-'Aas saying: "As Allâh is my witness," three times – placing his fingers in his ears – then he told that he heard Allâh's Messenger ﷺ saying:

"The Black Stone and the *Maqam* are two of the precious stones of Paradise. Allâh extinguished their light, and if He had not extinguished their light, they would have illuminated everything between the east and the west."[51]

---

[50] *At-Tirmidhi* (961).
[51] *Ahmad* (2/214) and *Ibn Khuzaimah* (2732).

When Ibrahim ﷺ was building the Ka'bah, one more stone was needed. Isma'il ﷺ wanted to go and get something, but Ibrahim ﷺ said, "Help me to find a stone as I told you to do." So, Isma'il ﷺ set out, looking for a stone, then he brought it to him and found that he had set the Black Stone in place. He said, "O my father, who brought you this stone?" He said, "It was brought to me by one who is not relying on you to build it. It was brought to me by Jibril from heaven."[52]

It was reported that 'Abdullah bin 'Umar ﷺ touched the Stone, then he kissed his hand and said: "I have never failed to do that since I saw Allâh's Messenger ﷺ kiss it."[53]

---

[52] Part of a *Hadith* narrated by 'Ali in *Tafsir Ibn Kathir* (1/258); *Tafsir At-Tabari* (143). It is *Mawquf* (untraceable, discontinued) with *Isnad* that stop at 'Ali , but it comes under the same ruling as a *Marfu'* (traceable) report.
[53] *Muslim* (1268).

The Well of Zamzam

The story of how it was dug and began to flow as a blessing for mankind is well known.

Ibrahim ﷺ brought the nursing infant Isma'il and his mother, and left them by a big tree above Zamzam. There were no plants in Makkah and no water. He left with her a bag containing dates and an old water-skin[54] filled with water, then he turned to leave. The mother of Isma'il followed him, and said, "Where are you going and leaving us in this valley where there is nobody and nothing?" She said that to him several times, and he did not turn towards her. Then she said, "Has Allâh commanded you to do this?" He said, "Yes." She said, "Then Allâh will not forsake us."

Then she went back, and Ibrahim ﷺ left. When he reached Ath-Thaniyah (mountain path), where they could not see him, he turned to face the House and prayed in the following words, raising his hands:

$$﴿رَّبَّنَآ إِنِّيٓ أَسْكَنتُ مِن ذُرِّيَّتِي بِوَادٍ غَيْرِ ذِى زَرْعٍ عِندَ بَيْتِكَ ٱلْمُحَرَّمِ رَبَّنَا لِيُقِيمُواْ ٱلصَّلَوٰةَ فَٱجْعَلْ أَفْئِدَةً مِّنَ ٱلنَّاسِ تَهْوِىٓ إِلَيْهِمْ وَٱرْزُقْهُم مِّنَ ٱلثَّمَرَٰتِ لَعَلَّهُمْ يَشْكُرُونَ﴾ [إبراهيم: ٣٧].$$

"O our Lord! I have made some of my offspring to

---

[54] Old water-skins kept water cooler than new ones.

dwell in an uncultivable valley by Your Sacred House (the Ka'bah at Makkah) in order, O our Lord, that they may perform *As-Salah* (*Iqamat-as-Salah*). So fill some hearts among men with love towards them, and (O Allâh) provide them with fruits so that they may give thanks." [*Ibrahim* 14:37]

The mother of Isma'il started to breastfeed Isma'il ﷺ and drink from that water, until it ran out and her son became thirsty. She started to watch him writhing – or rolling in the dust and writhing – then she went away, unable to look at him. She found As-Safa which was the closest mountain of the land nearby. She stood on top of the mountain and turned to face the valley, looking if she could see anyone, but she did not see anyone. Then she came down from As-Safa, and

when she reached the valley, she lifted the hem of her skirt and started running like one who is exhausted, until she crossed the valley, then she came to Al-Marwah and stood on top of it, and looked to see whether she could see anyone, but she did not see anyone. She did that seven times.

Ibn 'Abbas  narrated that the Prophet ﷺ said:

"This why the people run between them in *As-Sa'y*."

When she stood upon Al-Marwah (for the last time), she heard a voice and she said, "Shh!" telling herself to be quiet. Then she listened, and she heard it again. She said, "I can hear you, can you help us?" Then she saw an angel standing on the site of Zamzam. He started to scrape the ground with his heels – or with his wings – until water started to appear. She started to heap the earth up around it, doing like this with her hands, and she started to scoop some water into her water-skin. The water decreased after she had scooped some up.

Ibn 'Abbas narrated that the Prophet ﷺ said:

"If she had left Zamzam alone – or if she had not scooped up some of the water – Zamzam would have been a plentiful spring."

So, she drank and nursed her baby. The angel said to her: "Do not be afraid of being forsaken, for here will be the House of Allâh, which this boy and his father will build, and Allâh does not forsake His people."[55]

The Disappearance of Zamzam

Then Zamzam disappeared and all traces of it vanished with

---

[55] *Fath Al-Bari* (3364).

the passing of time.

Yaqut Al-Hamawi said in *Mu'jamul-Buldan*: "As the days passed, that flow ceased and no known trace of Zamzam remained. The correct view is that Jurhum are the ones who buried it when they left Makkah and went away."

'Abdul-Muttalib redug the Well of Zamzam

Zamzam remained hidden, its location unknown, until 'Abdul-Muttalib took charge of providing water for the pilgrims and looking after them. Someone came to him in his dream and said to him, "Dig *Tibah*." He said, "What is *Tibah*?" The next night he came to him (in his dream) and said, "Dig *Barrah*."[56] He said, "What is *Barrah*?" The next night he came to him again and said, "Dig *Al-Madnunah*."[57]

---

[56] It was called *Barrah* because of its many benefits.

[57] *Madmunah* means exclusive; it was so named because it is exclusively for the believers.

He said, "What is *Al-Madnunah* ?" Then it was said to him, "Dig Zamzam." He said, "What is Zamzam?" He said, "It is (a well) whose water does not dry up and with which no one can find fault; it will quench the thirst of a great number of pilgrims. It comes from between excretions and blood [*cf An-Nahl* 16:66], where the crow with whiteness in its wings pecks. It is an honor for you and your descendents."

The crow with whiteness in its wings was always present in the place where animals were butchered, a place of excrement and blood. So, the next day 'Abdul-Muttalib took a pick and shovel, and he took with him his son Al-Harith – at that time he had no other son. He dug for three days until he uncovered the well, then he said *"Allâhu Akbar*! This is the well of Isma'il."

Quraish said to him, "Give us a share in it." He said, "I will not do that; this is something that has been given to me exclusively. So, appoint whoever you want as judge between me and you." They chose the soothsayers of Banu Sa'd.

So, they set out to go to them, and they got so thirsty on the road that they thought they were going to die.

'Abdul-Muttalib said, "By Allâh, doing nothing is a sign of helplessness. Why do we not travel in the land, for perhaps Allâh will provide us with water." So, they rode on, then 'Abdul-Muttalib went to his mount and started riding, and when it started running, a spring of sweet water started to flow under its hooves. 'Abdul-Muttalib said, *"Allâhu Akbar."* His companions said likewise, and they all drank.

They said to him: "The One Who gave you water has passed judgement against us. By Allâh we will never dispute with

you concerning this." Then they went back and stopped arguing with him about Zamzam.[58]

The Names of Zamzam

Zamzam has many names, and a large number of names is indicative of the great status of the thing named. It was said that it is called Zamzam because its water is so plentiful, as the word *Zamzamah* in Arabic implies quantity and coming together. And it was said that it was called Zamzam because Hajrah (may peace be upon her) gathered (*Zummat*) the sand around it lest the water start to flow right and left; if she had left it, it would have flowed until it covered everything. Its names other than Zamzam include: *Al-Shabba'ah*, *Barrah*, *Tibah*, *Bushra*, *'Awnah*, *Safiyah*, *Sharab Al-Abrar*, *Madnunah* and other names.

---

[58] See *Muthir Al-Gharam*, reported by Ibn Ishaq in his *Maghazi* (1/24) and from him by Al-Azraqi in *Akhbar Makkah* (2/46), and by Al-Baihaqi in *Ad-Dala'il* (1/78).

The Water of Zamzam and its Virtues

There are many *Ahadith* and reports that affirm its virtues. One of the facts that affirm its virtues is that when Jibril عليه السلام opened the chest of Allâh's Messenger ﷺ, he washed his heart with Zamzam water. If there had been any better water, he would have washed the heart of the Chosen Prophet ﷺ with it.

Abu Dharr Al-Ghifari رضي الله عنه narrated that Allâh's Messenger ﷺ said:

> "The roof of my house was opened when I was in Makkah, and Jibril عليه السلام came down and opened my chest, then he washed it with Zamzam water. Then he brought a large bowl of gold filled with wisdom and faith, and poured it into my chest, and then he closed it up. Then he took me by the hand and took me up to the heavens."[59]

According to another *Hadith* narrated by Anas رضي الله عنه: Jibril عليه السلام came to Allâh's Messenger ﷺ when he was playing with other boys. He took hold of him and wrestled him to the ground, and then he took out his heart, split it open and took out a clot. He said, "This is the Satan's share of you." Then he washed it with Zamzam water, put it back together and put it back in its place. The children came running to his mother – i.e., his foster-mother – and said, "Muhammad has been killed!" So, they went out to see him and found him looking

---

[59] *Al-Bukhari* (3342).

pale. Anas ﷺ said: "I used to see the marks of the stitches on the Prophet's chest."[60]

Concerning the virtues of Zamzam water, Ibn 'Abbas ﷺ narrated that Allâh's Messenger ﷺ said:

> "The best water on the face of the earth is the water of Zamzam. In it is complete nourishment and healing from sickness. The worst water on the face of the earth is the water in Wadi Barahut in Hadramout. On its surface are vermin that look like the feet of locusts. It flows in the morning and dries up in the evening."[61]

Mujahid said: "I never saw Ibn 'Abbas ﷺ feed any people but he also offered them Zamzam water to drink."[62] He also said that whenever a guest came to stay, Ibn 'Abbas would honor him with Zamzam water.[63]

Another sign of its virtue is that Allâh's Messenger ﷺ said that drinking one's fill of Zamzam water was a sign of being free of hypocrisy.

Ibn 'Abbas ﷺ narrated that Allâh's Messenger ﷺ said:

> "A sign that distinguishes us from the hypocrites is that they do not have their fill of Zamzam water."[64]

---

[60] *Ahmad* (3/288) and *An-Nasa'i* (1/224).

[61] At-Tabarani, *Al-Kabir* (11167). It says in *Al-Majma'* that the men of its *Isnad* are *Thiqah* (reliable).(3/286)

[62] *Akhbar Makkah* (1117).

[63] *Akhbar Makkah* (1118).

[64] *Ad-Daraqutni* (2/288) and *Al-Baihaqi* (5/147). The men of its *Isnad* are *Thiqah* as Al-Busairi said, but there is some confusion with regard to 'Uthman as to the naming of his two Shaikhs. It was classed as *Da'eef* by Al-Albani in *Da'eef Ibn Majah*, 597. See also his comments in *Irwa'ul-Ghalil* (1125).

Note: It is *Mustahab* (desirable) to perform *Wudu'* etc., with it. It was narrated from Jabir ﷺ that the Prophet ﷺ called for a vessel of Zamzam water, and he drank from it and performed *Wudu'*.[65] According to Ahmad, the Prophet ﷺ did three circuits (of *Tawaf*) starting and ending at Al-Hijr, then he prayed two *Rak'ahs*, then he went back to the Hijr, then he went to Zamzam and drank from it and poured some water on his head."[66]

Zamzam is Healing

It is proven in the *Sahih Ahadith* that there is healing in the water of Zamzam. This is also proven from well-known stories, both ancient and modern, in which Allâh has healed people of disease, sometimes in cases where medicine had failed to do so and the doctors had despaired of the patient's recovery. Ibn 'Abbas ﷺ narrated that Allâh's Messenger ﷺ said:

> "The best water on the face of the earth is the water of Zamzam. In it is complete nourishment and healing from sickness."[67]

Allâh's Messenger ﷺ said:

> "The water of Zamzam is for the purpose for which it is drunk."[68]

So, whoever drinks it for the purpose of seeking healing, Allâh

---

[65] Classed as *Hasan* (fair) by Al-Albani in *Irwa'ul-Ghalil* (1124).

[66] *Ahmad* (3/394). Its *Isnad* are *Sahih* according to the conditions of Imam Muslim.

[67] At-Tabarani, *Al-Kabir* (11167).

[68] *Ibn Majah* (3062).

may heal him by His grace. Abu Hamzah said: I was keeping the people away from Ibn 'Abbas, and I did not come to see him for a few days. He said: "What kept you away?" I said: "(I had a) fever." He said: "Allâh's Messenger ﷺ said: 'Fever is a breeze from Hell, so cool it down with Zamzam water.'"[69]

Qais bin Kurkum said that he asked Ibn 'Abbas ﷺ: "Will you not tell me about Zamzam?" He said: "Its supply cannot be exhausted and it cannot be criticized. It is complete nourishment and healing from sickness. It is the best water that we know of."[70]

And it is Food

According to the *Hadith*:

"The water of Zamzam is for the purpose for which it

---

[69] *Ahmad*, 1/291; its *Isnad* are *Sahih* according to the conditions of the Two Shaikhs [Al-Bukhari and Muslim].
[70] *Akhbar Makkah* by Al-Fakihi (1098).

is drunk."

Abu Dharr ⚜ lived on it for an entire month, during which nothing entered his stomach but Zamzam water, but he did not feel any hunger. In *As-Sahih*, it is narrated:

> When Abu Dharr ⚜ became Muslim, he said, "O Messenger of Allâh, I have been here for thirty days and nights." He asked, "Who fed you?" He said, "I had no food apart from Zamzam water, but I gained so much weight that I could feel the folds of fat on my stomach, and I did not feel hungry at all." He said, "It is blessed and it provides complete nourishment."[71]

It was reported that Ibn 'Abbas ⚜ said concerning Zamzam: "We used to call it *Ash-Shabba'ah* (that which satisfies), the best help in providing for one's children."[72]

Stories of the healing of the Sick with Zamzam Water

There are dozens, indeed hundreds, of stories of how sick people were healed of diseases when the doctors had despaired of their recovery, but Allâh caused them to be healed by means of Zamzam water and its hidden benefits, and they were restored to full health. It is sufficient for us to cite just one example, from the modern era:

> This is a well known story from our own times, the main character of which is still living amongst us, confirming the story and telling of the Power of Allâh, affirming the truth of the Prophet's words that the

---

[71] *Muslim* (2473).
[72] *Majma'uz-Zawa'id* (3/286) and *'Abdur-Razzaq* (5/117).

water of Zamzam is for the purpose for which it is drunk, and that Zamzam water offers healing from sickness and complete nourishment. This is the story of Layla Al-Hilw, from Morocco. Layla was suffering from cancer. She had been neglectful of the remembrance of Allâh, proud of her good health and beauty. After she found out that she was sick, she went to Belgium, where she was told that she had no option but to have her breast removed and undergo chemotherapy, which would make her hair fall out and cause her to grow a beard, and it would also make her lose her nails and teeth. She refused this treatment and asked for less aggressive treatment, then she went back to Morocco. But after six months she had suffered a drastic loss of weight, her color had changed and she was wracked with pain, so she went back to Belgium, where the doctors told her husband that the disease had spread everywhere, even to her lungs, and that there was no medicine that could benefit her now. They advised him to take her home to die. But her husband remembered something that he had forgotten; Allâh inspired him to visit the Sacred House of Allâh. So he and his wife went there, and she wept a great deal when she saw the Ka'bah. She prayed to Allâh not to dash her hopes and to astound the doctors with her case. Layla started to read the Book of Allâh and to drink her fill of Zamzam water. She felt a sense of peace and tranquility in the House of Allâh. She asked her husband to let her stay in the *Haram* and not go back to the hotel. So, she stayed there in *I'tikaf* (seclusion). The upper half of her body was

filled with tumors and swellings that confirmed that the disease had spread. The women with her in the *Haram* advised her to keep washing her upper half with Zamzam water, but she was afraid to touch the tumors on her body. Finally she put her fears aside and started to wipe with Zamzam water her body and breasts that were filled with blood and pus. Then the unexpected happened: all the tumors disappeared and there was no more pain or pus. Allâh had healed her by means of the hidden benefits of Zamzam water. Allâh's Messenger ﷺ indeed spoke the truth when he said:

"In it is complete nutrition and healing from sickness."

Al-Multazam

Al-Multazam is the space between the *Rukn* and the door of the Ka'bah. It was reported that Mujahid said: "The area between the *Rukn* and the door is Al-Multazam. Whoever calls upon Allâh in Al-Multazam, Allâh will answer his prayer."[73]

It was reported that 'Abdullah bin 'Abbas 🙏 used to cling (*Yalzam*) to the space between the *Rukn* and the door, and he used to say: "The area between the *Rukn* and the door is called Al-Multazam; no one clings to it asking Allâh for anything, but it will be given to him."[74]

Ibn Al-Qaiyim said concerning the Prophet's standing at Al-Multazam: "What is narrated is that he did that on the day of the conquest of Makkah. In *Sunan Abi Dawud* it is reported that 'Abdur-Rahman bin Abi Safwan said: "When Allâh's Messenger 🙏 conquered Makkah, I went out and saw that Allâh's Messenger 🙏 had come out of the Ka'bah, he and his Companions. They touched the *Rukn* from the door to the Hatim (a space between the Black Stone and the door of the Ka'bah), pressing their cheeks against the House, and Allâh's Messenger 🙏 was in their midst."[75]

---

[73] Its *Isnad* are *Hasan*. It was reported by Al-Azraqi in *Tarikh Makkah* (2/368).

[74] Its *Isnad* are *Hasan*. It was reported by Al-Baihaqi in *Al-Kubra* (5/164).

[75] Reported by Abu Dawud (1898). His *Isnad* include Yazid bin Abi Ziyad Al-Hashimi who is *Da'eef* (weak), but the rest of its men are *Thiqah*; the following reports corroborate it and lend it strength.

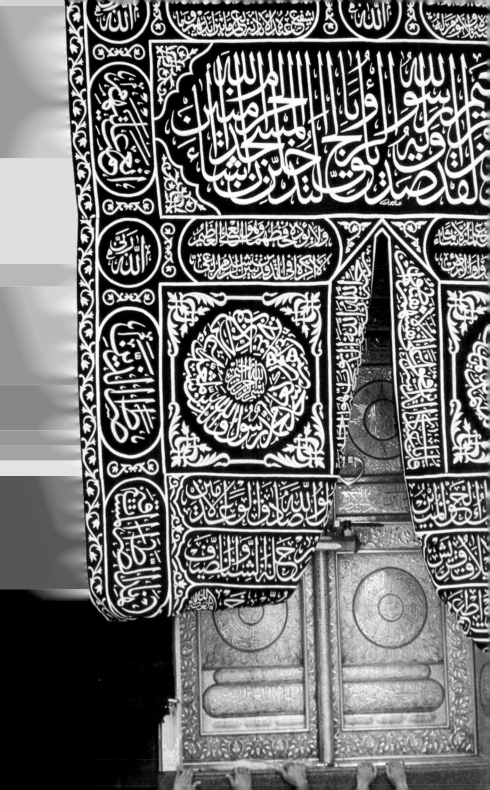

Abu Dawud also reported from 'Amr bin Shu'aib, from his father from his grandfather, who said: "I did *Tawaf* with 'Abdullah, and when he was parallel with the back of the Ka'bah, I said: 'Will you not seek refuge with Allâh.' He said: 'We seek refuge with Allâh from the Fire.' Then he went on until he touched the Black Stone, then he stood between the *Rukn* and the door, placing his chest, face and forearms like this (spreading them out), he said: 'I saw Allâh's Messenger 彌 doing like this.'"[76]

This may be understood as referring to the time of the Farewell *Tawaf* or to some other time. But Mujahid, Ash-Shafi'i and others said that it is *Mustahab* to stand at the Multazam after doing *Tawaf Al-Wada'* (Farewell *Tawaf*) and pray to Allâh.[77]

Many *Ahadith* report that the *Sahabah* used to cling to Al-Multazam and make *Du'a'* there. It was reported that Abu Az-Zubair said: "I saw 'Abdullah bin 'Umar, Ibn 'Abbas and 'Abdullah bin Az-Zubair clinging to Al-Multazam."[78] And it was reported that Hanzalah said: "I saw Tawus seeking refuge with Allâh between the Black Stone and the door."[79]

'Uthman bin Al-Aswad said that Mujahid saw a person between the door and the *Rukn*, so he struck him on the shoulder – or on his back – and said: "*Ilzam, ilzam* (cling, cling)." Marwan said in his *Hadith*: Mujahid said: "The space between the *Rukn* and the door is called Al-Multazam,

---

[76] Reported by Abu Dawud (1899); its *Isnad* include Al-Muthanna bin As-Sabah, who is *Da'eef*, but it is supported by the preceding report.
[77] *Zadul-Ma'ad* (2/218).
[78] *Akhbar Makkah* by Al-Fakihi (233). Its *Isnad* are *Hasan*.
[79] *Akhbar Makkah* by Al-Fakihi (232).

and it is very rare that Allâh is asked for something there or refuge is sought with Him from something, and He does not respond."[80]

It was reported that Tariq bin 'Abdur-Rahman said: "I did *Tawaf* with 'Ali bin Al-Husain, and when he had finished his *Tawaf*, he lowered his *Izar* (lower garment) until his stomach was showing, then he pressed it against the area between the *Rukn* and the door."[81]

---

[80] Its *Isnad* are *Sahih*. It was reported by 'Abdur-Razzaq (5/76).
[81] Its *Isnad* are *Hasan*. *Akhbar Makkah* by Al-Fakihi (242).

The Conquest of Makkah

When the treaty of Al-Hudaibiyah was completed, Khuza'ah sided with the Messenger ﷺ and Banu Bakr sided with Quraish. But a man from Banu Bakr killed a man from Khuza'ah, and as a result war broke out between the two sides. Quraish supplied Banu Bakr with weapons, and some of Quraish even fought alongside Banu Bakr under cover of darkness. In this manner they broke their agreement with Allâh's Messenger ﷺ. Some people from Khuza'ah came to seek support from Allâh's Messenger ﷺ, so he commanded the people to get ready and told them that he was heading for Makkah. He said, "O Allâh. Do not let Quraish find out about our plans until we take them by surprise in their own land." Then the people got ready.

When Allâh's Messenger ﷺ had set out for Makkah, Hatib bin Abi Balta'ah wrote a letter to Quraish, informing them of what Allâh's Messenger ﷺ had decided to do and how he had commanded the Muslims to set out towards Makkah. Then he gave the letter to a woman and paid her wage to deliver it to Quraish. She put it on her head and wrapped her braids around it, and then she set out. Allâh's Messenger ﷺ received news from heaven about what Hatib had done, so he sent 'Ali bin Abi Talib ؓ and Az-Zubair bin Al-'Awwam ؓ and told them: "Catch up with the woman with whom Hatib has sent the letter to Quraish, warning them about what we have decided to do in their case." So, they set out until they caught

up with her in Rawdah Khakh at the place[82] of Banu Abi Ahmad. They told her to dismount and they looked in her saddlebags, but they did not find anything.

'Ali bin Abi Talib ⬥ said to her: "I swear that Allâh's Messenger was not told lies and we were not told lies. Either you bring this letter forth for us or we will expose you." When she saw that they meant it, she said: "Turn away from me." So, he turned away and she undid her braids and brought forth the letter and gave it to him. He took it to Allâh's Messenger ﷺ who called Hatib to him and said: "O Hatib, what made you do this?" He said: "O Messenger of Allâh, by Allâh I still believe in Allâh and His Messenger, and I have not changed. But I am a man who has no family or clan among the people, and I have a child and a wife among them, so I tried to do (Quraish) a favor for their sake." 'Umar bin Al-Khattab ⬥ said: "O Messenger of Allâh, let me strike his neck (i.e., kill him), for the man is a hypocrite!" Allâh's Messenger ﷺ said: "How do you know, O 'Umar, perhaps Allâh looked at the people of Badr on the day of Badr and said: 'Do what you like, for I have forgiven you.'"[83]

Allâh's Messenger ﷺ set out on the tenth of Ramadan, and Quraish did not know anything about it. No news reached them of Allâh's Messenger ﷺ and his army. Abu Sufyan bin Harb went out with Hakim bin Hizam and Budail bin Warqa' to try and find out what was happening. Al-'Abbas ⬥, the paternal uncle of the Prophet ﷺ, had gone out to Al-Arak, riding the white mule of Allâh's Messenger ﷺ, hoping to

---

[82] Yaqut said: this place was a station twelve miles from Al-Madinah on the way to Diyar Sulaim.

[83] *Al-Bidayah wan-Nihayah* (6/521).

meet those who were coming to Makkah, to tell them where Allâh's Messenger ﷺ was, so that they might come to him and ask him for protection. Al-'Abbas ؓ met Abu Sufyan and advised him to ride with him and go and ask Allâh's Messenger ﷺ for protection. So, he went with him, and Allâh's Messenger ﷺ invited him to embrace Islam and he did so. After he became Muslim, Al-'Abbas ؓ said: "O Messenger of Allâh, Abu Sufyan is a man who likes to have status, so give him something." He said: "Yes, whoever enters the house of Abu Sufyan, will be safe. Whoever closes his door will be safe. Whoever enters the Sacred Mosque will be safe."[84]

When Allâh's Messenger ﷺ entered Dhu Tuwa, he bowed his head in submission to Allâh when he saw how Allâh had honored him by enabling him to conquer Makkah, and he lowered his head so much that the hair of his beard was almost touching the middle of his saddle.

The Armies enter Makkah

Each detachment of the army set out to do as Allâh's Messenger ﷺ had commanded it to do.

Khalid ؓ and his troops did not engage in any fighting, apart from what happened with regard to Banu Bakr and the *Ahabesh* (tribes living in suburbs) at the bottom of Makkah, whom they fought and Allâh caused them to defeat them. Safwan bin Umaiyah, 'Ikrimah bin Abi Jahl and Suhail bin 'Amr had gathered some people to fight in Al-Khandamah. When the Muslims, the companions of Khalid bin Al-Walid ؓ, encountered them, they skirmished with them;

---

[84] *Seerat Ibn Hisham* (4/37).

approximately twelve or thirteen of the *Mushrikun* (polythiests) were killed, and they were defeated. Allâh's Messenger ﷺ had instructed the Muslim commanders, when he ordered them to enter Makkah: "Do not kill anyone except those who fight you," – except for a few whom he mentioned by name, who he said were to be killed even if they were found beneath the curtain of the Ka'bah. These included 'Abdullah bin Sa'd bin Abi Sarh, 'Abdullah bin Khatal, the two singing-girls of 'Abdullah bin Khatal, Al-Huwairith bin Nuqaidh bin Wahb, Miqyas bin Subabah, 'Ikrimah bin Abi Jahl, and Sarah the slave woman of some of Banu 'Abdul-Muttalib. Of these people, 'Abdullah bin Khatal, Miqyas bin Subabah, and one of the two singing-girls of Ibn Khatal were killed. The rest asked for protection and Allâh's Messenger ﷺ granted them that.

The Prophet ﷺ entered Makkah with those who were with him, from Adhakhir. That was on Friday the 19th of Ramadan in the year mentioned.[85] This was stated by Al-'Ulaimi in *Tarikh Al-Quds*. In *Tuhfatul-Kiram bi Akhbar Baladillâhil-Haram* by Al-Fasi it is reported from Al-Waqidi that Allâh's Messenger ﷺ came on Friday when there remained 10 nights of Ramadan."

A tent was pitched for him in Al-Abtah, and he entered on his she-camel Al-Qaswa', riding between Abu Bakr and Usaid bin Hudair ﷺ, and he stayed at his tent in Al-Abtah. Ibn 'Umar ﷺ said:

When the Prophet ﷺ entered Makkah on the day of the Conquest, he saw women brushing the dust from the

---

[85] 8 AH.

horses' faces with their veils. Abu Bakr smiled and the Prophet ﷺ said: "O Abu Bakr, what does Hassan say?" Abu Bakr recited the words of Hassan bin Thabit :

"May I lose my dear daughter, if you do not see her,

Wiping away the dust from the two sides of Kada' [a hill near Makkah]

They pull at the reins, going upward

Our women wipe them with their veils."[86]

﴿ جَآءَ ٱلْحَقُّ وَزَهَقَ ٱلْبَطِلُ إِنَّ ٱلْبَطِلَ كَانَ زَهُوقًا ﴾

[الإسراء: ٨١]

When the people had calmed down, the Prophet ﷺ came out, riding his she-camel, until he reached the Ka'bah. He did seven circuits of *Tawaf*, riding his camel, and touching the Black Stone each time with a stick that had a curved top. Around the Ka'bah there were three hundred and sixty idols fixed to the ground with lead. The idols fell on their faces as he started poking them, saying:

﴿ جَآءَ ٱلْحَقُّ وَزَهَقَ ٱلْبَطِلُ إِنَّ ٱلْبَطِلَ كَانَ زَهُوقًا ﴾ [الإسراء: ٨١] .

"Truth (i.e., Islamic Monotheism or this Qur'ân or *Jihad* against polytheists) has come and *Batil* (falsehood, i.e., Satan or polytheism) has vanished. Surely, *Batil* is ever bound to vanish." [Al-Isra' 17:81]

---

[86] *Mana'ihul-Karam*, 1/485, 486.

According to the *Hadith* of Jabir 🙵: We entered Makkah with Allâh's Messenger 🙵, and in or around the House there were three hundred and sixty idols which were worshipped instead of Allâh. Allâh's Messenger 🙵 commanded that they were all to be made to fall on their faces, and then he said:

"Truth (i.e., Islamic Monotheism or this Qur'ân or *Jihad* against polytheists) has come and *Batil* (falsehood, i.e., Satan or polytheism) has vanished. Surely, *Batil* is ever bound to vanish." [*Al-Isra'* 17:81]

According to Al-Bukhari, when Allâh's Messenger 🙵 came to Makkah, he refused to enter the House when there were gods in it. He ordered that they should be brought out, and they brought out (statues of) Ibrahim and Isma'il with *Azlam* (arrows for seeking good luck or for decision-making) in their hands. Allâh's Messenger 🙵 said:

"May Allâh curse them (Quraish), for by Allâh they knew that they (Ibrahim and Isma'il) never draw lots with these arrows."

Then he entered the House, proclaimed Allâh's Greatness in each corner, but he did not pray inside.[87] The correct view, however, is that he did pray inside the Ka'bah, as it says in the *Hadith* of Ibn 'Umar 🙵 reported by Al-Bukhari.[88] After the Prophet 🙵 had prayed inside the Ka'bah, he walked about inside the House, proclaiming the Greatness and Oneness of Allâh. Then he opened the door, and Quraish had filled the mosque and stood there in rows, waiting to see what he would do. He stood holding onto the sides of the doorway,

---

[87] *Al-Bukhari* (1601).
[88] *Al-Bukhari* (1599).

﴿ يَـٰٓأَيُّهَا ٱلنَّاسُ إِنَّا خَلَقْنَـٰكُم مِّن ذَكَرٍ وَأُنثَىٰ وَجَعَلْنَـٰكُمْ شُعُوبًا وَقَبَآئِلَ لِتَعَارَفُوٓاْ إِنَّ أَكْرَمَكُمْ عِندَ ٱللَّهِ أَتْقَنكُمْ إِنَّ ٱللَّهَ عَلِيمٌ خَبِيرٌ ﴾ [الحجرات:١٣]

with them standing below him, and said:

"None has the right to be worshipped but Allâh, He has no partner or associate. He has made good His Promise and helped His slave. He alone put to flight the Confederates. Every claim of privilege or blood or property is abolished by me except the custody of the sanctuary and the watering of the pilgrims. The unintentionally slain in a quasi-intentional way by club or whip, for him the blood money (*Diyah*) is more severe; a hundred camels, forty of them to be pregnant. O Quraish, Allâh has taken from you the pride of the *Jahiliyah* and its pride in ancestry. Man sprang from Adam and Adam sprang from dust."

Then he recited the Verse:

﴿ يَـٰٓأَيُّهَا ٱلنَّاسُ إِنَّا خَلَقْنَـٰكُم مِّن ذَكَرٍ وَأُنثَىٰ وَجَعَلْنَـٰكُمْ شُعُوبًا وَقَبَآئِلَ لِتَعَارَفُوٓاْ إِنَّ أَكْرَمَكُمْ عِندَ ٱللَّهِ أَتْقَنكُمْ إِنَّ ٱللَّهَ عَلِيمٌ خَبِيرٌ ﴾

"O mankind! We have created you from a male and a female, and made you into nations and tribes, that you may know one another. Verily, the most honorable of you with Allâh is that (believer) who has *At-Taqwa* [i.e., he is one of the *Muttaqun* (the pious)]. Verily, Allâh is All-Knowing, All-Aware." [*Al-Hujurat* 49:13]

Then he said: "O Quraish, what do you think I am going to do
with you?" They said: "Good, for you are a noble brother,
son of a noble brother." He said: "I say to you what Yusuf
(Joseph) said to his brothers:

'No reproach on you this day.' [*Yusuf* 12:92]

Go, for you are free."

Then Allâh's Messenger ﷺ gave the keys of the Ka'bah back
to 'Uthman bin Talhah, whom he had commanded to bring
them.

The People's Oath of Allegiance to Allâh's Messenger ﷺ

After the conquest, the people gave their oath of allegiance
to Allâh's Messenger ﷺ. Allâh's Messenger ﷺ sat at Qarn
Masqalah[89], and the people came to him, young and old,

---

[89] This is a place-name. Masqalah was a man who lived there during the
Jahiliyah.

History of Makkah

men and women, and gave their oath of allegiance based on faith and the testimony that none has the right to be worshipped but Allâh.

When the Prophet ﷺ had finished receiving the men's oath of allegiance, he accepted the women's oath of allegiance whilst he was atop As-Safa, with 'Umar ﷺ sitting beneath him, receiving their oath of allegiance on behalf of the Prophet ﷺ. They gave their oath of allegiance based on the pledge that they would not associate anything with Allâh, they would not steal, they would not commit adultery, they would not kill their children, they would not utter slander intentionally forging falsehood (i.e., by making illegal children belonging to their husbands), and they would not disobey him (the Prophet ﷺ) in any *Ma'ruf* (Islamic monotheism and all that which Islam ordains). [*cf Al-Mumtahanah* 60:12]

The Length of the Prophet's Stay in Makkah and some of the Important Things that He did

The Prophet ﷺ stayed in Makkah for nineteen days, and during the whole period he shortened his prayers. The place where he stayed and where a tent was pitched for him was Shi'b Abi Talib, Allâh's Messenger ﷺ did many things during the days of the conquest of Makkah, some of which we have mentioned already, such as breaking the idols which were around the Ka'bah, praying inside the House, erasing the pictures that were inside it, affirming that custody of the Ka'bah belonged to Banu Shaibah and that the right to provide water for the pilgrims belonged to Banu 'Abdul-Muttalib. He also commanded Bilal ﷺ to call the *Adhan* (call for prayer) from atop the Ka'bah; he proclaimed that some of

the most bitter enemies were to be killed; he accepted the oath of allegiance from both men and women; he commanded Abu Usaid Al-Khuza'i to renew the boundary markers of the *Haram*; and he sent out parties to call people to Islam because he knew that the conquest of Makkah would make many of those who had been hostile towards Islam more prepared to accept it.

He also sent out parties to destroy the idols. He sent Khalid ﷺ to break the idol of Al-'Uzza which was in Nakhlah (a place near Makkah). This took place on the twenty-fifth of Ramadan in 8 AH. Al-'Uzza belonged to Quraish and Banu Kinanah, and it was the greatest of their idols. And the Prophet ﷺ sent 'Amr bin Al-'Aas to break Suwa', the idol of Hudhail; and he ﷺ sent Sa'd bin Zaid Al-Ashhali to break Manat in Ramadan of the eighth year after the *Hijrah* of Allâh's Messenger ﷺ.

The Ban on the *Mushrikun* entering Al-Masjid Al-Haram

After Allâh's Messenger ﷺ returned from the conquest of Makkah, delegations kept on coming to Al-Madinah to announce their Islam. The time for *Hajj* approached, but the Messenger ﷺ could not go out to lead the Muslims on *Hajj*. Delegations were coming one after another, but there were still people in the Arabian Peninsula who did not believe in Allâh and His Messenger ﷺ. There were still some *Kuffar* and Jews there, and the *Kuffar* – as had been the case during the *Jahiliyah* – were still performing pilgrimage to the Sacred House during the sacred months. The *Kuffar* were impure, so it was more appropriate that the Messenger ﷺ stay

in Al-Madinah until Allâh completed His Word and until He gave him permission to perform pilgrimage to His House. So, Abu Bakr ﷺ went out to lead the people on *Hajj*.

The *Mushrikun* were also still performing pilgrimage to the Sacred House of Allâh, so it was essential to cleanse the Ka'bah of the visits of the *Mushrikun*, just as it had recently been cleansed of idols and idolatry.

At the end of Dhul-Qa'dah in 9 AH, Abu Bakr As-Siddiq ﷺ went out with the permission of Allâh's Messenger ﷺ to lead the *Hajj*. He took with him twenty *Badanah* (camels) to sacrifice on behalf of Allâh's Messenger ﷺ and fifty on behalf of himself. There were with him three hundred men of Al-Madinah. When he reached Dhul-Hulaifah, seven miles from Al-Madinah, Allâh's Messenger ﷺ sent 'Ali bin Abi Talib ﷺ after him to tell him to recite *Surat Bara'ah* (*At-Taubah*) concerning the *Mushrikun*, in which it says:

﴿يَـٰٓأَيُّهَا ٱلَّذِينَ ءَامَنُوٓا۟ إِنَّمَا ٱلْمُشْرِكُونَ نَجَسٌ فَلَا يَقْرَبُوا۟ ٱلْمَسْجِدَ ٱلْحَرَامَ بَعْدَ عَامِهِمْ هَـٰذَا وَإِنْ خِفْتُمْ عَيْلَةً فَسَوْفَ يُغْنِيكُمُ ٱللَّهُ مِن فَضْلِهِۦٓ إِن شَآءَ إِنَّ ٱللَّهَ عَلِيمٌ حَكِيمٌ﴾ [التوبة:٢٨].

"O you who believe (in Allâh's Oneness and in His Messenger Muhammad ﷺ)! Verily, the *Mushrikun* (polytheists, pagans, idolaters, disbelievers in the Oneness of Allâh, and in the Message of Muhammad ﷺ) are *Najasun* (impure). So, let them not come near Al-Masjid Al-Haram (at Makkah) after this year; and if you fear poverty, Allâh will enrich you if He wills,

out of His Bounty. Surely, Allâh is All-Knowing, All-Wise." [*At-Taubah* 9:28]

Allâh commanded His believing slaves, who are pure in spiritual and religious terms, to expel the *Mushrikun*, who are impure in religious terms, from Al-Masjid Al-Haram, and not to let them approach it after this Verse was revealed. 'Ali ﷺ called out on the Day of *Al-Adha*: "O people! After this year no *Mushrik* should perform *Hajj*, no one should perform *Tawaf* around the House naked, but for those who have a treaty with Allâh's Messenger ﷺ, they are granted a respite according to the terms of their treaties."

 The people were given a respite of four months after that, to allow each people to return to its land. But from that day no *Mushrik* performed *Hajj*, and no one performed *Tawaf* around the House naked. The *Mushrikun* started to wonder and asked one another: "What will you do now that Quraish has become Muslim?" Then they too became Muslim.

expanded it on the Syrian and western sides.

This expansion was started in Muharram 137 AH, and ended in Dhul-Hijjah 140 AH. The area added by Al-Mansur was half as much again as it had been previously.[91]

The Addition of Al-Mahdi

Then it was expanded by Al-Mahdi bin Abi Ja'far Al-Mansur, from the highest point and on the Yemeni side, and from where his father had stopped on the western side.

He did two expansions. The first was in 161 AH, in which he added two porticos to what his father had added.

The second was in 167 AH, for which he had issued orders when he did his second *Hajj* in 164 AH, but this addition was not completed until the reign of his son Musa Al-Hadi, because Al-Mahdi died before it could be completed.

Al-Mahdi spent huge amounts of money on the expansion

---

[91] See *Shifa'ul-Gharam* by Al-Fasi (1/426).

and development of *Al-Masjid Al-Haram*, because he allocated for every broken column inside the Mosque a value of twenty-five dinars. He brought marble columns from Syria and other places, which were unloaded at Jeddah and transported from there to Makkah on wheels, and he did other things that added up to great expense.[92]

The Addition of Dar An-Nadwah

Then Dar An-Nadwah was added to the mosque. The one who was behind this idea wrote to the minister of the Abbasid Caliph Al-Mu'tadid – 'Ubaidullâh bin Sulaiman bin

Wahb – suggesting to him that he should incorporate the remaining part of Dar An-Nadwah into the Mosque, and telling him that this was a great honor and an opportunity that had not been available to any caliph after Al-Mahdi. The one who was behind this idea had asked the *Qadi* of Makkah, Muhammad bin Ahmad Al-Muqaddami, and its governor,

---

[92] See *Shifa'ul-Gharam* by Al-Fasi (1/427).

'Ajj bin Haj (the freed slave of Al-Mu'tadid), to write similar letters concerning Dar An-Nadwah. So, they also wrote letters, and their letters were shown to Al-Mu'tadid. Al-Mu'tadid issued orders that Dar An-Nadwah should be turned into a mosque and joined to *Al-Masjid Al-Haram*, and he spent a great deal of wealth on that. So, Dar An-Nadwah was knocked down and a mosque was built on its foundations, with columns, small windows and porticos roofed with teak adorned with gold. Then twelve doors were made in the wall of the Great Mosque, and three doors were made opening onto the street around it, and minarets and balconies were added. This work was completed in three years, and it may have been completed in 284 AH.[93]

The Gate of Ibrahim

The addition that is known as the Gate of Ibrahim was done during the reign of Al-Muqtadir Billah Al-'Abbasi in 306 AH. The Gate of Ibrahim is on the western side of the Mosque. This addition is of the courtyard that is located between the Tailors' Gate and the Gate of Banu Jumah, and links them together. The courtyard was incorporated into the Mosque and the two gates were replaced with one large gate, which was called *Bab Ibrahim* (the Gate of Ibrahim).[94]

This marks the final stage in the development of *Al-Masjid Al-Haram* undertaken by the 'Abbasid Caliphs. The next stage of development, renovation and repairs done to the

---

[93] See *Shifa'ul-Gharam* by Al-Fasi (1/430).
[94] The Ibrahim referred to here is not the Prophet Ibrahim u, rather he was a tailor who used to sit in front of this gate, so it was known by his name. *Mana'ihul-Karam* (2/186).

Mosque took place under the reign of the Sultan Saleem in 979 AH.

The Development of Sultan Saleem

There was a fire in the Mosque in 802 AH, during the reign of Sultan Barquq, the Sultan of Egypt. Sultan Barquq repaired it and restored the roof made of wood and teak. These repairs were made repeatedly, and the structure became weakened. This was reported to Sultan Saleem, who issued orders that it should be knocked down and rebuilt, and that it should not be given a wooden roof; rather it should be roofed with domes. This work was started in 979 AH, and it was completed by his son Sultan Murad III in 984 AH.

Expansion of Al-Masjid Al-Haram during the Saudi Era

The area of the Mosque remained as it had been during the reign of Al-Muqtadir Billah for 1069 years, but construction around the Mosque did not cease, in fact it kept growing closer until houses and buildings were actually attached to the Mosque. Similar developments happened in the *Mas'a* (area where *Sa'y* is performed), until there were buildings in between, separating the *Mas'a* from the Mosque, leaving a narrow street surrounded by shops and multi-storied houses.

The Mosque became too small for the pilgrims in its restricted courtyards, for the number of pilgrims was no longer as it had been before, in the days of pack animals and sailing boats. The numbers multiplied greatly because of the developments in means of transportation and the introduction of modern cars, jet planes and steamships. The Mosque was too small for such great numbers of people, and as years went by, the numbers of pilgrims increased and the overcrowding became more severe. Residents and pilgrims alike felt the pressure on space in Makkah, and it is strange indeed that not one of the kings or rulers of the Muslims thought of adding even a single hand span to the area of the Mosque for over one thousand years.

Beginning of Expansion

The good news that a start was to be made on expansion came when it was announced that the expansion of the

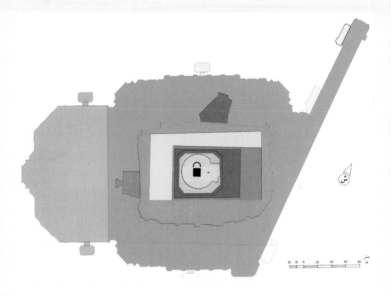

Prophet's Mosque, which had begun in 1370 AH, had been completed. On that occasion an official announcement was made stating that orders had been issued for all the tools and equipment that had been used in the expansion of the Prophet's Mosque would now be moved to Makkah Al-Mukarramah to make an immediate start on the expansion of *Al-Masjid Al-Haram*. This announcement was broadcast on 5th Muharram 1375 AH.

The First Expansion – 1375 AH/1956 CE

King 'Abdul-'Aziz bin 'Abdur-Rahman Aal Sa'ud (may Allâh have mercy on him and reward him greatly on behalf of Islam) took a keen interest in the affairs of the two Sacred Mosques. Based on this, he issued commands that the Mosque should be repaired, which included paving it with marble, repainting it and repairing the doors and floors of the porticos. He was the first one to pave the *Mas'a* (place of

History of Makkah

Sa'y) and renew its roof.[95]

The first expansion during the Saudi era was during the reign of King Sa'ud bin 'Abdul-'Aziz, who knocked down both levels of houses on both sides of the *Mas'a*. On the first level he added a low barrier to separate the people traveling in opposite directions, from As-Safa to Al-Marwah and coming back from Al-Marwah to As-Safa. He added sixteen doors on the lower level, and two entrances to the upper level, one of them at As-Safa and the other at Al-Marwah. Then he knocked down the buildings on the southern side, and built a new two-level portico. He also built a level of basements underneath the expansion but not underneath the *Mas'a*. Then he completed the expansion on the western and northern sides in a similar manner to his expansion on the southern side. He added a number of doors, bringing the total to fifty-one, including large and small ones. He also built seven minarets to replace the seven old minarets, which has been destroyed during the expansion.

The area added during the first Saudi expansion added up to 153,000 square meters, bringing the total area of the Mosque to 180, 850 square meters, thus increasing the area of the mosque sixfold. Before this expansion the Mosque had covered only 27,850 square meters.

The new expansion was well built and fine looking, as the walls were covered with marble, and the roofs and pillars with artificial stone, making the Mosque a work of art and an architectural wonder.

---

[95] The first one who made a roof over the *Mas'a* to provide shade was King Ash-Sharif Al-Husain bin 'Ali in 1339 AH.

The Expansion of King Fahd bin 'Abdul-'Aziz Aal Sa'ud (may Allâh protect him) – 1409 AH/1988 CE

The Custodian of the Two Holy Mosques, King Fahd bin 'Abdul-'Aziz Aal Sa'ud (may Allâh protect him) took a deep interest in the sanctuary and spent a great deal of money on it. His projects, which have been carried out, had two aims:

1. Improvement and upgrading
2. Increasing the area of the Mosque

With regard to increasing the area, an addition was made on the western side, which extends from the King 'Abdul-'Aziz Gate to the 'Umrah Gate, including two upper levels and a basement. He also prepared the roof of the mosque so that people may offer prayer there. The roof is considered to be a true addition as it may contain more than 80,000 worshippers. After the roof was improved and prepared, and with the addition of three escalators, it is like having added a third level to the two previous levels. The expansion also included a major gate, which is the King Fahd Gate, plus fourteen minor gates, and entrances to the basements. This brings the number of principal gates of *Al-Masjid Al-Haram* to four, and the number of minor entrances to fifty-four, besides six entrances to the basements and the upper entrances to the second level and the escalators.

Two new minarets were also added, which resemble the previous seven minarets.

The area covered by this extension is 76,000 square meters, which is three times the area of Al-Masjid Al-Haram before

the first Saudi extension. This means that the two Saudi expansions together increased the area of the Mosque ninefold. New areas have been added for worshippers on the eastern side of the Mosque, next to the *Mas'a*. This is known as *As-Sahah Ash-Sharqiyah* (the eastern courtyard), located at the bottom of Jabal Abi Qubais. This area covers approximately 40,000 square meters. It has been equipped with everything that the worshippers need. This is in addition to spacious areas on the southern and western sides that are paved with white marble, to accommodate a larger number of worshippers, especially at the time of *Hajj*.

Unification of the Prayer Halls of the *Haram*

Uniting all the worshippers in the *Haram* behind a single *Imam* is a matter that is no less important than expanding and improving the *Haram* and preparing it for the worshippers; indeed it is far more important. Before the prayers were

united behind one *Imam*, there used to be different prayer stations in the *Haram*, one for Imam Malik, one for Imam Ash-Shafi'i, one for Imam Ahmad bin Hanbal and one for Imam Abu Hanifah, and in each of these prayer stations there was an *Imam* who would lead people in prayer. The *Adhan*

would be given once, but then the prayers in each station would be done at different times. First the prayer would be done at the station of Imam Ahmad, then when it was over, the prayer would be done at the station of Imam Ash-Shafi'i, then at the station of Imam Malik, and finally at the station of Imam Abu Hanifah, and each station had its own *Imam*. This arrangement was set up by the Ottomans, and this odd situation continued until the time of King 'Abdul-'Aziz bin 'Abdur-Rahman Aal Sa'ud (may Allâh have mercy on him), who was keen to remove all negative features from the lives of Muslims, and to restore things to the way they had been at the time of Allâh's Messenger ﷺ and the righteous *Salaf*. So, he commanded that the Muslims should be united behind one *Imam*.

Historical Sites in Makkah

Jabal Hira'

Jabal Hira' (the Mount of Hira') was singled out for many blessings. Allâh honored it by making it the place where the Prophet ﷺ often stayed, and where the Revelation first came to him. The Revelation came to the Prophet ﷺ in a cave in Hira'. This cave is at the top of Hira', towards the back of the mountain. It is a cave that is well known to the people, knowledge of which was passed down from one generation to another. Allâh's Messenger ﷺ used to go there to worship, before the Revelation came to him. It was reported that 'Aishah ﷺ said:

> "The onset of the Divine Inspiration (*Wahy*) that came to Allâh's Messenger ﷺ, was in the form of good dreams; he did not see a dream but it would come true like the break of day. Then solitude was made dear to him, so he used to go alone to the cave of Hira' and devote himself to worship there for several nights before coming back to his family. He would take with him provisions for his stay, then he would go back to Khadijah ﷺ and take a similar amount of provisions…"[96]

Jabal Hira' was honored and blessed in a way that happened to no other mountain. It is one of the most blessed places

---

[96] *Al-Bukhari.*

because, besides Allâh's Messenger ﷺ having spent so much time there, it also witnessed the beginning of the revelation to Allâh's Messenger ﷺ.

According to the *Hadith* narrated by 'Aishah ﵞ, (he stayed there) until the truth came to him suddenly when he was in the cave of Hira'. He said:

"The angel came and said, 'Read!' I said, 'I do not know how to read.' He took hold of me and pressed me so hard that I could not bear it any more. Then he released me and said, 'Read!' I said, 'I do not know how to read.' He took hold of me a second time and pressed me so hard that I could not bear it any more. Then he released me and said, 'Read!' I said, 'I do not know how to read.' He took hold of me a third time and pressed me so hard that I could not bear it any more. Then he released me and said, 'Read!…'"[97]

Allâh's Messenger ﷺ and his Companions would sometimes climb Jabal Hira' after his Mission began. It was reported that Abu Hurairah ◈ said:

"Allâh's Messenger ﷺ was on a rock on Hira', he and Abu Bakr, 'Umar, 'Uthman, 'Ali, Talhah and Az-Zubair. The rock moved, and Allâh's Messenger ﷺ said, 'Be still, for there is no one on you but a Prophet, a Siddiq or a martyr.'"[98]

Jabal Thawr

This is at the bottom of Makkah, and it is the place where Allâh's Messenger ﷺ and Abu Bakr ◈ hid when they migrated to Al-Madinah. They hid in a well-known cave in the mountain. This is the cave to which Allâh referred in His Book when He said:

$$﴿ ثَانِيَ ٱثۡنَيۡنِ إِذۡ هُمَا فِي ٱلۡغَارِ ﴾ الآية [التوبة: ٤٠]$$

"…the second of the two; when they (Muhammad ﷺ and Abu Bakr ◈) were in the cave," [At-Taubah 9:40]

---

[97] This is part of the previous *Hadith*.
[98] *Muslim* (2417) and *Ahmad* (2/419).

– i.e., at the time of the *Hijrah* when the *Mushrikun* plotted to kill him, detain him or expel him, so he fled from amongst them, accompanied by his close friend Abu Bakr As-Siddiq ﷺ, and hid in a cave for three days until his pursuers had given up and gone back, then they went on to Al-Madinah. Abu Bakr ﷺ started to worry that someone would find them and cause harm to the Prophet ﷺ, but the Prophet ﷺ reassured him and said to him:

"O Abu Bakr, what do you think of two people when Allâh is the third one with them?"[99]

[99] *Al-Bukhari* (3653).

It was narrated from Anas 🙵 that Abu Bakr 🙵 told him:

"I was with the Prophet 🙵 in the cave, and I saw the footsteps of the *Mushrikun*. I said, 'O Messenger of Allâh, if one of them were to lift his foot he would see us.' He said, 'What do you think of two people when Allâh is the third one with them?'"[100] This cave is well known in this mountain; knowledge of it has been passed down from one generation to another, and people go there to visit it.

---

[100] *Al-Bukhari* (4663).

Masjid Al-Khaif and its Virtues

This is one of the mosques whose virtues are proven in some *Ahadith* and reports. According to the *Marfu'* (traceable) *Hadith* of Ibn 'Abbas :

"Seventy Prophets prayed in Masjid Al-Khaif."[101]

The Prophet ﷺ prayed there during his *Hajj*, and the Companions of Allâh's Messenger ﷺ acknowledged the virtues of this mosque, and spoke very highly of it, and encouraged the people to pray there when performing the rituals of *Hajj*.

It was reported that Ibn Juraij said: "I said to 'Ata': 'A merchant was busy selling during the days of *Hajj*, and he was not able to pray there until he had completed the *Hajj*.'

---

[101] *Majma'uz-Zawa'id* (3/297); this was classed as *Hasan* (fair) by Al-Albani in

He said, 'Let him pray there.' I said, 'Is it obligatory to pray there?' He said, 'No, but pray there if you can.'"

Abu Hurairah ﷺ said: "If I were one of the people of Makkah, no Friday would come without me praying there."[102]

There is no *Sahih Hadith* that proves that seventy Prophets are buried in this mosque; all reports to that effect are *Da'eef* (weak).

The Graveyard of Al-Mu'alla

In Makkah there are many graveyards, including that which is known as Al-Mu'lla. Al-Azraqi said: The people of Makkah used to bury their dead on the two sides of the valley, *Yumnah* and *Shamah*, both during the *Jahiliyah* and after the advent of Islam. Then they moved all their graves to Ash-Shi'b Al-Aisar.

Al-Azraqi told that his grandfather said: "We do not know of any valley in Makkah that faces the Ka'bah directly except the valley of the graveyard, which faces the Ka'bah along its entire length.

Many of the Companions, their successors, major scholars and righteous people were buried in this graveyard, yet despite that no precise location is known for the graves of any of the Companions, and there is nothing to show that the grave which is said to be that of Khadijah bint Khuwailid ﷺ is in fact her grave.[103] And Allâh knows best.[104]

---

[102] *Al-Manasik* (p. 39). *Akhbar Makkah* by Al-Fakihi (4/271). The editor said: its *Isnad* are *Hasan*, and the report of Abu Hurairah ﷺ also has *Hasan Isnad*.

[103] The correct view is that she is buried in Al-Abwa', which is between Al-Madinah and Makkah, approximately 13 miles from Rabigh.

[104] *Shifa'ul-Gharam* (1/535).

Mina

This is the place in which the pilgrims are commanded to stay until the sun rises on Thabir mountain on the day of *'Arafah*, and on the Day of Sacrifice and the days of *At-Tashriq* which follow it. In Mina the pilgrims stone the *Jamarat* (stone pillars representing the *Shaytan*). Mina is filled with people during the *Hajj* season, but is almost empty for the rest of the year, apart from the people who live there.

The boundary of Mina extends from the villages of Wadi Muhassar to Al-'Aqabah which is the location of the *Jamrah* which is closest to Makkah, namely *Jamratul-'Aqabah* where Allâh's Messenger ﷺ accepted the oath of allegiance (*Bai'ah*) of the *Ansar*.

Among the virtues of Mina is that this is where Masjid Al-Khaif is located, and that this is where Allâh sent the ram to Ibrahim عليه السلام as a ransom for his son, the story of which is well known.

'Arafat

'Arafah is also known as 'Arafat. Standing in 'Arafat is an essential part of the *Hajj*; whoever misses the standing in 'Arafat has missed *Hajj*, because the Messenger ﷺ said:

"*Hajj* is '*Arafah*."

In that case one has to make up *Hajj* the following year and offer a sacrifice (*Hady*). The day of '*Arafah* has many virtues, as was narrated in many *Ahadith*.

'Aishah ﷺ said that Allâh's Messenger ﷺ said:

"There is no day on which Allâh frees more slaves from the Fire than the day of '*Arafah*. He comes close, then He praises them to the angels saying: 'What do these (people) want?'" [105]

Allâh's Messenger ﷺ said:

"The *Shaytan* is never seen on a day when he is smaller, more insignificant, more defeated and more

---

[105] *Muslim* (1348); *Ibn Majah* (3014); *An-Nasa'i* (3003) and others.

annoyed than on the day of *'Arafah*, and that is only because of what he sees of mercy coming down and Allâh forgiving great sins."[106]

It was reported that Tariq bin Shihab said: A man from among the Jews came to 'Umar and said: "O *Amirul-Mu'minin*, there is a Verse in your Book which, if it had been revealed to us Jews, we would have taken that day as a festival." He said: "Which Verse?" He said:

﴿ ٱلۡيَوۡمَ أَكۡمَلۡتُ لَكُمۡ دِينَكُمۡ وَأَتۡمَمۡتُ عَلَيۡكُمۡ نِعۡمَتِى وَرَضِيتُ لَكُمُ ٱلۡإِسۡلَٰمَ دِينًا ﴾ [المائدة: ٣].

"This day, I have perfected your religion for you, completed My Favor upon you, and have chosen for you Islam as your religion." [Al-Ma'idah 5:3]

'Umar said: "We know the day and the place in which that was revealed to the Prophet ﷺ; it was when he was standing

---

[106] *Malik* (2/395); *'Abdur-Razzaq* (4/378); *Al-Fakihi* (5/26) and others.

in *'Arafah*, on a Friday."[107]

One of the virtues of the day of *'Arafah* is that fasting this day expiates for the sins of the past and coming year. It was reported from Abu Qatadah that a man said:

"O Messenger of Allâh, what do you think of fasting the day of *'Arafah*?" He said: "I hope that Allâh will expiate for the sins of the past and coming year."[108]

Muzdalifah

Muzdalifah is the place where the pilgrims are commanded to stay overnight after leaving 'Arafat at night. It is the place between the two *Ma'zims* (narrow mountain paths) of 'Arafat and Muhassir. The *Ma'zim* of 'Arafat is the place which is called *Al-Madiq* (narrow passage). A number of scholars gave this definition, including Ash-Shafi'i in his book *Al-Umm*, where he says: "The boundary of Muzdalifah extends from the two *Ma'zims* of 'Arafat, until one comes to Qarn

---

[107] *Al-Bukhari* (45) and *Muslim* (3017).
[108] *Muslim* (1162) and *At-Tirmidhi* (752).

Muhassir, and on your right and left in this area everything you can see, the mountain passes and trees, are all part of Al-Muzdalifah."

Muzdalifah is also called Jam', and it is so called because the people gather (*Ijtima'*) there. It is also *Al-Mash'ar Al-Haram* which Allâh mentioned in His Book, when He said:

﴿ فَإِذَآ أَفَضۡتُم مِّنۡ عَرَفَٰتٍ فَٱذۡكُرُواْ ٱللَّهَ عِندَ ٱلۡمَشۡعَرِ ٱلۡحَرَامِۖ ﴾ الآية [البقرة:١٩٨].

"Then when you leave 'Arafat, remember Allâh (by glorifying His Praises, i.e., prayers and invocations) at the *Mash'ar Al-Haram*." [*Al-Baqarah* 2:198]

Some said that *Al-Mash'ar Al-Haram* is a part of Muzdalifah, not all of it. In the lengthy *Hadith* of Jabir ﷺ there is an indication that *Al-Mash'ar Al-Haram* is a part of Muzdalifah and not all of it, because in this *Hadith*, after mentioning that the Prophet ﷺ stayed in Al-Muzdalifah overnight and prayed *Fajr* there, he mentions that he then rode Al-Qaswa (his she-camel) until he came to *Al-Mash'ar Al-Haram*, then he turned to face the *Qiblah*, and made *Du'a*, proclaiming the Greatness and Oneness of Allâh, whilst standing.

Staying overnight in Muzdalifah is obligatory, and whoever does not do it must offer a sacrifice. It is *Mustahab* to follow the example of Allâh's Messenger ﷺ in staying overnight until *Fajr* comes, than stand there until daybreak. But there is nothing wrong with the weak and women setting out earlier, and going on to Mina before sunrise.

Al-Muhassir

This is a place through which it is recommended to hurry. It is a valley between Mina and Muzdalifah at the end of both but is not a part of them. It is called Al-Muhassir because when the people reach it during their *Hajj*, they say "*La ilaha illallâh*" there and walk quickly through the valley that is connected to it. The reason why it is *Mustahab* to hasten through this place is that this was what the Prophet ﷺ did there.

He did that because it is a dwelling place of *Shayatin* (devils), so he regarded it as *Mustahab* to hasten through it.

Al-Muhassab[109]

It is *Mustahab* (desirable) for the pilgrims to stop in Al-Muhassab after leaving Mina. It is in Makkah on the way to Mina; this is the place where Allâh's Messenger ﷺ stopped. It was narrated from Abu Rafi' – who was in charge of the luggage of the Prophet ﷺ that he said:

"The Prophet ﷺ did not command me to stop in Al-Abtah, but I pitched his tent for him there, and he came and stayed there."

'Aishah ﷺ said:

"The Prophet ﷺ stopped there because it was easier for him when he wanted to leave, so whoever wanted to, could stop there; and whoever did not want to, did not do so."[110]

Ibn Juraij said: I used to hear the people say to 'Ata': "The

---

[109] Al-Muhassab is a water course between Makkah and Mina.
[110] See *Akhbar Makkah* by Al-Azraqi.

قَالَ النَّبِيُّ صَلَّى اللهُ عَلَيْهِ وَسَلَّمَ لِعَبْدِ الرَّحْمَنِ:
أَرْدِفْ أُخْتَكَ ـ يَعْنِي عَائِشَةَ ـ فَأَعْمِرْهَا
مِنَ التَّنْعِيمِ ..... الْحَدِيثَ

Prophet ﷺ stopped there that night to wait for 'Aishah ﵃." He would say, "No, rather it was a place for the caravans to spend the night," and he would say, "whoever wants to camp there, may do so; and whoever does not want to, does not have to."

Masjid At-Tan'im

It is also known as the Mosque of 'Aishah *Ummul-Mu'minin* (Mother of the believers) because it is in the place where she went to enter *Ihram* for *'Umrah*, when the Messenger ﷺ told her to do so during the Farewell Pilgrimage. In the lengthy *Hadith* of Jabir bin 'Abdullah ﵃ it says:

> 'Aishah ﵃ was menstruating, so she performed all the rituals, except for *Tawaf* around the House. When her period had ended and she had done *Tawaf*, she said: "O Messenger of Allâh, how come you have done *'Umrah* and *Hajj*, and I have done *Hajj* only?" So, he ordered 'Abdur-Rahman bin Abu Bakr (i.e., her brother) to go with her to al-Tan'im, where she entered *Ihram* after doing *Hajj* in Dhul-Hijjah.[111]

The mosque is situated 7.5 km from *Al-Masjid Al-Haram*, on

---

[111] *Al-Bukhari* (1785).

﴿ وَأَنَّ ٱلْمَسَٰجِدَ لِلَّهِ فَلَا
تَدْعُوا۟ مَعَ ٱللَّهِ أَحَدًا ﴾

the road from Makkah Al-Mukarramah to Al-Madinah Al-Munawwarah, which is known as *Tareeq Al-Hijrah*. It is considered to be one of the outstanding features of Makkah because of its unique Islamic design and distinct construction.[112]

Masjid Al-Ji'ranah[113]

Al-Ji'ranah is a well between At-Ta'if and Makkah, closer to Makkah. The Prophet ﷺ stopped there when he divided the booty of Hawazin, on the way back from the campaign of Hunain, and he entered *Ihram* from there. There is a mosque there that is known as Masjid Al-Ji'ranah.

Abul-Abbas Al-Qadi said: "The best of *'Umrah* for the people of Makkah and its vicinity is from Al-Ji'ranah, because Allâh's Messenger ﷺ did *'Umrah* from there."[114]

It was narrated from Al-Zinji that Ibn Juraij said: "Ziyad bin

---

[112] *Ad-Dalil Al-Irshadi lil-Haj*, 1415 AH, published by the Ministry of Islamic Affairs and Awqaf (p. 24); *Akhbar Makkah* by Al-Azraqi (vol. 2, p. 208).
[113] Al-Ji'ranah; it is also known as Al-Ji'irranah to scholars of *Hadith*.
[114] *Mu'jamul-Buldan* (2/166).

Muhammad bin Tariq told me that he did *'Umrah* with Mujahid from Al-Ji'ranah, and he entered *Ihram* from behind the valley where a stone is set up, and he said, 'From here the Prophet ﷺ entered *Ihram*.''[115]

Taqiuddin Al-Fasi reported that the Prophet ﷺ entered *Ihram* from the mosque which is beneath the *Wadi* in Al-'Udwah Al-Quswa in Al-Ji'ranah, which was the place where the Prophet ﷺ offered prayer when he was in Al-Ji'ranah. He entered *Ihram* on the night of Wednesday 18th Dhul-Qa'dah, and he went to Al-Ji'ranah on the night of Thursday 5th Dhul-Qa'dah, so he stayed there for thirteen days.[116]

Al-Ji'ranah is the best of the *Miqats* for starting *'Umrah* from Makkah, because the Prophet ﷺ entered *Ihram* from that place, according to the *Madhhab* of Malik, Ash-Shafi'i, Ibn Hanbal and other scholars, may Allâh be pleased with them.

عَنْ مُحَرِّشٍ الْكَعْبِيِّ رَضِي الله عَنْهُ: أَنَّ رَسُولَ الله صَلَّى اللهُ عَلَيْهِ وَسَلَّمَ خَرَجَ مِنَ الْجِعْرَانَةِ مُعْتَمِرًا فَدَخَلَ مَكَّةَ لَيْلًا ثُمَّ خَرَجَ مِنْ تَحْتِ لَيْلَتِهِ فَأَصْبَحَ بِالْجِعْرَانَةِ كَبَائِتٍ .... الْحَدِيثُ

---

[115] *Shifa'ul-Gharam* (1/546).
[116] *Shifa'ul-Gharam* (1/546).

Masjid Al-Jinn (the Mosque of the Jinn)

This is on the edge of Al-Hajun, and is built on the place where Allâh's Messenger ﷺ drew a line for 'Abdullah bin Mas'ud ؓ. The Prophet ﷺ had been commanded to recite the Qur'ân to the jinn, so he took Ibn Mas'ud ؓ with him and went to Al-Hajun, near Shi'b Abi Dubb.

It was narrated from Ibn 'Uthman that 'Abdullah bin Mas'ud ؓ said:

Allâh's Messenger ﷺ offered *'Isha'* prayer, then he went away. He took Ibn Mas'ud ؓ by the hand and went out with him, until they came to the bottom of the valley of Makkah, where he sat him down and drew a line around him. Then he said to him: "Do not leave, woe to you. For some men will come to you, but do not talk to them and they will not talk to you." Then Allâh's Messenger ﷺ went away until I could not see him, and whilst I was sitting like that, I saw some men who looked like *Az-Zut*,[117] their hair and bodies looked like them but I could not see their private parts or their skin. They kept coming up to the line but they did not cross it; then they went to Allâh's Messenger ﷺ, then towards the end of the night Allâh's Messenger ﷺ came and found me inside the line. He said: "These people annoyed me this night." Then he entered the line with me, and he put his head on my thigh and slept. When he used to sleep the sound of his breathing could be heard.[118]

---

[117] *Az-Zut*: a kind of black or Indian people.
[118] *Al-Bukhari* (8).

Hajj (Pilgrimage)

Hajj is one of the pillars of Islam, one of its basic principles and obligations. This is indicated by the Qur'ân, the *Sunnah* and scholarly consensus. It is *Fard 'Ain* (an individual obligation) upon every accountable person who is able to do it, once in a lifetime. Whoever denies that has committed *Kufr* (disbelief). There is a great deal of evidence that *Hajj* is obligatory, including the following:

From the Qur'ân:

﴿ وَلِلَّهِ عَلَى ٱلنَّاسِ حِجُّ ٱلْبَيْتِ مَنِ ٱسْتَطَاعَ إِلَيْهِ سَبِيلًا ۚ وَمَن كَفَرَ فَإِنَّ ٱللَّهَ غَنِيٌّ عَنِ ٱلْعَٰلَمِينَ ﴾ [آل عمران:٩٧].

Allâh says:"And *Hajj* (pilgrimage to Makkah) to the House (Ka'bah) is a duty that mankind owes to Allâh, those who can afford the expenses (for one's conveyance, provision and residence); and whoever disbelieves [i.e., denies *Hajj* (pilgrimage to Makkah), then he is a disbeliever of Allâh], then Allâh stands not in need of any of the *'Alamin* (mankind, jinn and all that exists)" [Aal-'Imran 3:97]

﴿ وَأَتِمُّوا۟ ٱلْحَجَّ وَٱلْعُمْرَةَ لِلَّهِ ﴾ [البقـرة:١٩٦].

"And perform properly (i.e., all the ceremonies according to the ways of Prophet Muhammad ﷺ), the

Hajj and *'Umrah* (i.e. the pilgrimage to Makkah) for Allâh." [*Al-Baqarah* 2:16]

From the *Sunnah*:

'Abdullah bin 'Umar ﷺ narrated that Allâh's Messenger ﷺ said:

> "Islam is built on five (pillars): the testimony that none has the right to be worshipped but Allâh and that Muhammad is Allâh's Messenger; establishing regular prayer; paying *Zakah*; fasting Ramadan; and performing Pilgrimage to the House for whoever is able to do so."[119]

Whoever has not performed *Hajj* and is able to do so, must hasten to do it, because the Prophet ﷺ said:

> "Hasten to do *Hajj* – meaning the obligatory *Hajj* – for you do not know what will happen to you."[120]

Many texts have been narrated concerning the virtues of *Hajj*; we cannot quote them all here, but we will quote some of them:

Allâh's Messenger ﷺ said:

> "Do you not know that Islam wipes out that which came before it (of sin), *Hijrah* (migration for the sake of Allâh) wipes out that which came before it and *Hajj* wipes out that which came before it."[121]

---

[119] *Ahmad* (1/314).

[120] *Muslim* (121).

[121] *Al-Bukhari* (1819) and *Muslim* (1350).

And he ﷺ said:

> "Whoever performs pilgrimage to this House and does not have sexual relations (with his wife) or commit sin [*cf Al-Baqarah* 2:197], will come back (free of sin) as the day his mother bore him."[122]

And he said:

> "For an accepted *Hajj* there is no less a reward than Paradise."

When a Muslim resolves to travel for *Hajj* or *'Umrah*, it is *Mustahab* for him to write his will, and he must hasten to repent, meeting the well-known conditions of repentance which are: giving up the sin, regretting what has happened in the past, resolving not to return to it, and restoring the rights of anyone whom he has wronged. The pilgrim must choose good money [i.e., earned from *Halal* (lawful) sources] to spend on his *Hajj* and *'Umrah*, and he should travel in the company of good people. He should have knowledge of the rituals, and he should strive not to harm or annoy anyone. He must avoid any kind of obscenity, sin, disobedience to Allâh and arguments except those that are needed to support the truth. Women must not travel unless accompanied by a *Mahram* (a person forbidden to marry with).

The *Miqats* of *Ihram*

The *Miqats* are of two kinds – the *Miqat* of time and the *Miqat* of place. The *Miqat* of time starts at the beginning of Shawwal and ends on tenth night of Dhul-Hijjah, and it is

---

[122] *Al-Bukhari* (1773) and *Muslim* (1349).

permissible to enter *Ihram* one day before.

There are five *Miqats* of place:

 1. Dhul-Hulaifah for the people of Al-Madinah.[123]

 2. Al-Juhfah for the people of Syria.[124]

 3. Qarn Al-Manazil for the people of Najd.

 4. Yalamlam for the people of Yemen.

 5. Dhat 'Irq for the people of Iraq

The obligations of *Ihram*

 1. To enter *Ihram* from the *Miqat*

 2. To avoid sewn garments in the case of men.

Whoever neglects one of the obligations must offer a sacrifice.

The *Sunnahs* of *Ihram*

 1. Doing *Ghusl* and applying perfume.

 2. Wearing the two *Ihram* garments – the *Izar* (waist-wrapper or lower garment) and *Rida'* (upper garment).

 3. Cutting the nails.

 4. Reciting the *Talbiyah* repeatedly.

 5. Entering *Ihram* after offering a prayer.

***Hajj* of a Minor**

Hajj is not obligatory for a child who has not yet reached puberty, but if he performs *Hajj*, he will be rewarded; however, he will still have to perform the obligatory *Hajj* when he grows up. If a minor is of the age of discretion, he should make the intention for himself, as instructed by his guardian, who should tell him to do as much of the actions of

---

[123] The people enter *Ihram* nowadays from Rabigh.

[124] It is called Al-Sail nowadays

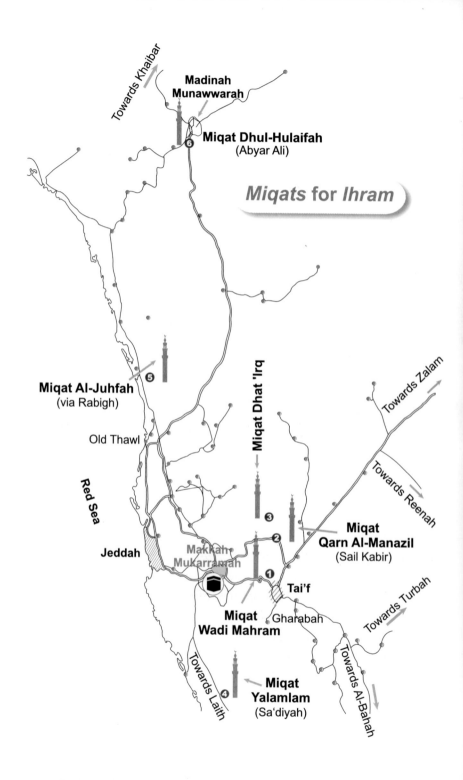

Miqats for *Ihram*

Towards Khaibar

Madinah Munawwarah

Miqat Dhul-Hulaifah
(Abyar Ali)

⑥

Towards Zalam

Miqat Al-Juhfah
(via Rabigh)

⑤

Old Thawl

Miqat Dhat 'Irq

Towards Reenah

Red Sea

③

②

Miqat Qarn Al-Manazil
(Sail Kabir)

Jeddah

Makkah Mukarramah

①

Tai'f

Towards Turbah

Miqat Wadi Mahram

Gharabah

Towards Laith

④

Miqat Yalamlam
(Sa'diyah)

Towards Al-Bahah

Hajj as he is able. As for the things he is unable to do, such as stoning the *Jamarat*, his guardian should do that on his behalf. If the minor is below the age of discretion, his guardian should form the intention on his behalf and take him to the different places of *Hajj*, and make him do what he can, and the guardian should do whatever the child, whether male or female, is unable to do. If the child is unable to do *Tawaf* or *Sa'y*, he should be taken for *Tawaf* and *Sa'y*, carried by others. It is preferable not to do both *Tawafs* and *Sa'ys* together, rather for the guardian to do them for himself first and then on behalf of the child. The rulings on *Ihram* for a minor are the same as the rulings on *Ihram* for adults.

Things that are prohibited during *Ihram*

The things that are prohibited are of different kinds:

1. Those which are forbidden for males and females alike:
1. Removing hair.
2. Cutting the nails.
3. Using perfume after entering *Ihram*.
4. Intercourse and whatever leads to it, such as getting married, looking with desire, kissing, etc.
5. Wearing gloves.
6. Killing game.

2. Those which are forbidden for men only:
1. Wearing sewn garments.
2. Covering the head.

3. That which is forbidden for women only:

There is only one thing that is forbidden for women, namely

Niqab (veil), i.e., it is forbidden for a women to wear over her face something that is sewn.

If a person does any of these prohibited actions with no valid excuse, then he must offer a *Fidyah* (expiation or ransom) and he has sinned. If he does it because of some need, then he must offer a sacrifice but he is not guilty of sin. If he does one of these forbidden things but he is excused for a reason such as ignorance, forgetfulness or being forced to do it, then there is no sin on him and he does not have to offer a sacrifice.

The Amount of the *Fidyah* (Expiation or Ransom)

The *Fidyah* for touching with desire, wearing sewn garments, removing hair, cutting nails, covering the head (for men), wearing *Niqab* (for women), wearing perfume or wearing gloves, is either sacrificing a sheep or feeding six poor persons or fasting three days – the person has the choice of doing any one of these three things, with no order of priority.

The *Fidyah* for omitting one of the obligatory duties of *Hajj*, such as stoning the *Jamarat*, staying overnight in Muzdalifah, staying overnight in Mina, doing *Tawaf Al-Wada'*, or entering *Ihram* from the *Miqat*, is to offer a sacrifice. If one cannot find an animal to sacrifice then he must fast for ten days, three during *Hajj* and seven when he returns to his family. If he is not able to fast three days during *Hajj* then he may fast them with the seven days after he returns to his family.

The Penalty for Hunting

If the animal he hunted has an equivalent, then he is given the

choice of slaughtering the equivalent animal and giving all of its meat to the poor of Makkah or of paying the equivalent value of the animal in food to be given to the poor, half a *Sa'* to each poor person fed or of fasting one day for each poor person he could have fed.

If the animal he hunted has no equivalent then he is given the choice between two things; either he should look at the equivalent value of the animal killed and give that in food to the poor, half a *Sa'* for each poor person or he should fast one day for each poor person he could have fed.

Obligation of offering the *Hady* (Sacrifice) for those who are doing *Tamattu'* and *Qiran*

Those who are doing *Tamattu'* or *Qiran*, must bring a *Hady* (sacrificial animal); if they cannot find an animal, they must fast for ten days, three during *Hajj* and seven when they return to their families.

The *Fidyah* to be given by one who is prevented from doing *Hajj* if he cannot find a *Hady*

He must offer a *Hady*; if he cannot find an animal, he must fast for ten days, as in the case of one who does *Tamattu'* or *Qiran*.

The *Fidyah* for having intercourse or doing any of the things that lead to it

The one who has intercourse before the first stage of exiting from *Ihram* must offer a *Badanah* (camel); if he cannot find an animal to sacrifice then he must fast for ten days, three during *Hajj* and seven when he returns to his family.

The Pillars and Obligatory Duties of *Hajj*[125]

A) The pillars of *Hajj*, of which there are four according to the sound scholarly opinion:

1. *Ihram*, which is the intention of starting the rituals. Whoever omits this intention cannot have entered the state of *Hajj*, because the Prophet ﷺ said:

"Actions are but by intention, and every man will have that which he intended."[126]

2. Standing in 'Arafat, because the Prophet ﷺ said:

"*Hajj* is *'Arafah*."[127]

3. *Tawaf Al-Ifadah*, because Allâh says:

﴿ وَلۡيَطَّوَّفُواْ بِٱلۡبَيۡتِ ٱلۡعَتِيقِ ﴾ [الحج: ٢٩].

"…and circumambulate the Ancient House (the Ka'bah at Makkah)." [*Al-Hajj* 22:29]

And because of the *Hadith* of 'Aishah ﷺ in which she tells

---

[125] *Murshidul-Mu'tamir wal-Hâjj waz-Za'ir* by Sa'eed bin 'Ali Al-Qahtani.

[126] *Al-Bukhari* (1) and *Muslim* (1907).

[127] Reported by the Five and others; classed as *Sahih* by Al-Albani in *Irwa'ul-Ghalil* (4/256).

the story of Safiyah 🕮.[128]

4. *Sa'y* between As-Safa and Al-Marwah, because the Prophet ﷺ said:

"Do *Sa'y*, for Allâh has prescribed *Sa'y* for you."[129]

And because of the *Hadith* of 'Aishah 🕮.[130]

B) Obligatory duties of *Hajj*

1. Entering *Ihram* from the *Miqat*, because when the Prophet ﷺ defined the *Miqats*, he said:

"...They (the *Miqats*) are for them (the people of the regions mentioned) and for whoever comes through them who is not resident there, and wants to perform *Hajj* or *'Umrah*."[131]

2. Standing at 'Arafat until sunset for those who stand there during the day, because the Prophet ﷺ stood there until sunset.[132]

3. Staying overnight in Muzdalifah, because the Prophet ﷺ stayed overnight there, and he said:

"Let my *Ummah* learn these rituals, for I do not know if I will meet them again after this year."[133]

---

[128] *Al-Bukhari* (1757) and *Muslim* (1211).

[129] *Ahmad* (6/421), *Al-Hakim* (4/70) and others; classed as *Sahih* by Al-Albani in *Irwa'ul-Ghalil* (4/269).

[130] *Muslim* (1277), *Al-Bukhari* (1709, 4495).

[131] *Al-Bukhari* (1845) and *Muslim* (1181).

[132] See the *Hadith* of Jabir ﷺ describing the *Hajj* of the Prophet , in *Sahih Muslim* (1218).

[133] This version is reported by *Ibn Majah* (3023); *Muslim* reported it with the words: "Learn these rituals..."

He permitted the weak to leave after midnight, which indicates that staying overnight in Muzdalifah is obligatory, and Allâh has commanded us to remember Him at *Al-Mash'ar Al-Haram*[134]

4. Staying overnight in Mina during the days of *At-Tashriq*, because the Prophet ﷺ stayed there overnight, and because he gave Al-'Abbas ﷺ permission to stay in Makkah during the nights when the people stay in Mina because of his task of providing water for the pilgrims,[135] and he allowed the camel herders to spend the night away from Mina.[136]

5. Stoning the *Jamarat* in order: *Jamratul-'Aqabah* on the Day of Sacrifice, and all three *Jamarat* on the days of *Tashriq*, because the Prophet ﷺ started with *Jamratul-'Aqabah*, and he stoned all three *Jamarat* on the three days of *Tashriq*. And because Allâh says:

﴿ ۞ وَٱذْكُرُواْ ٱللَّهَ فِىٓ أَيَّامٖ مَّعْدُودَٰتٖۚ فَمَن تَعَجَّلَ فِى يَوْمَيْنِ فَلَآ إِثْمَ عَلَيْهِ وَمَن تَأَخَّرَ فَلَآ إِثْمَ عَلَيْهِ لِمَنِ ٱتَّقَىٰۗ ﴾ [البقرة:٢٠٣].

"And remember Allâh during the Appointed Days. But whosoever hastens to leave in two days, there is no sin on him and whosoever stays on, there is no sin on him, if his aim is to do good." [Al-Baqarah 2:203]

---

[134] *Al-Bukhari* (1678, 1856) and *Muslim* (1293).

[135] *Al-Bukhari* (1745) and *Muslim* (1315).

[136] Because of the narrations reported by the Five. See *Irwa'ul-Ghalil* (4/28); *Wajibatul-Hajj Ma'al-Adillah wat-Ta'lil fi Sharhil-'Umdah* by Ibn Taimiyah (2/602-648).

And because of the *Hadith* of Jabir. [137]

6. Shaving the head or cutting the hair, because the Prophet ﷺ enjoined this and said:

"Let him cut his hair and exit *Ihram*."[138]

And because the Prophet ﷺ prayed three times for those who shaved their heads and one time for those who cut their hair.[139]

7. *Tawaf Al-Wada'* (Farewell *Tawaf*), because the Prophet ﷺ enjoined that:

"No one should leave and go home until the last thing he does has to do with the House (Ka'bah)."[140]

And because Ibn 'Abbas ﷺ said: "The people were told that the last thing they do should have to do with the House, but an exception was made for menstruating women."[141]

Whoever omits something that is an essential part of the rituals, and whoever omits an obligatory duty, must make up for it by offering a sacrifice. Whoever omits a *Sunnah* does not have to do anything.[142]

The evidence that the one who omits an obligatory duty must offer a sacrifice is, the words of Ibn 'Abbas ﷺ: "Whoever forgets or omits part of the rituals must offer a sacrifice."[143]

[137] *Muslim* (1297).
[138] *Muslim* (1227).
[139] *Al-Bukhari* (1727) and *Muslim* (1302).
[140] *Muslim* (1327).
[141] *Al-Bukhari* (1755) and *Muslim* (1328).
[142] See *Sharh Al-'Umdah* by Ibn Taimiyah (2/654), *Manarus--Sabil* (1/263) and *Hashiyatur-Rawd* by Ibn Qasim (4/204).
[143] *Al-Muwatta'* (1/419), *Ad-Daraqutni* (2/244), *Al-Baihaqi* (5/152); Al-Albani said that this was proven in a *Mawquf* report. See *Irwa'ul-Ghalil*

The Pillars and Obligatory Duties of *Umrah*

A) There are three pillars of *'Umrah*:[144]

1. *Ihram*, which is the intention of starting *'Umrah*, ecause of the *Hadith*

"Actions are but by intentions."[145]

2. *Tawaf*.

3. *Sa'y*. The Prophet ﷺ said concerning *Tawaf* and *Sa'y*:

"Whoever among you had not brought a *Hady* (sacrifice), let him perform *Tawaf* around the House and (do *Sa'y*) between As-Safa and Al-Marwah."[146]

And he ﷺ said concerning *Sa'y*:

"Do *Sa'y*, for Allâh has prescribed *Sa'y* for you."[147]

B) There are two obligatory duties of *'Umrah*:

1. Entering *Ihram* for it from outside the sanctuary, because the Prophet ﷺ commanded 'Aishah ﵂ to do *'Umrah* from At-Tan'im,[148] and because of the *Hadith* of Ibn 'Abbas ﵁ about the *Miqats*.

2. Shaving the head or cutting the hair, because the Prophet ﷺ said:

"Let him cut his hair and exit *Ihram*."[149]

---

[144] See *Hashiyatur-Rawd* (4/203) and *Manarus-Sabil* (1/261).

[145] *Al-Bukhari* (1) and *Muslim* (1907).

[146] *Al-Bukhari* (1691) and *Muslim* (1227).

[147] *Ahmad* (6/422), *Al-Hakim* (4/70) and others; classed as *Sahih* by Al-Albani in *Irwa'ul-Ghalil* (4/269).

[148] *Al-Bukhari* (1783) and *Muslim* (1211).

[149] *Al-Bukhari* (1691) and *Muslim* (1227).

Whoever omits an essential part of the *'Umrah*, his *'Umrah* is incomplete until he does it, and whoever omits one of its obligatory duties, must make up for it by offering a sacrifice. Whoever had intercourse before cutting his hair or shaving his head in *'Umrah* must sacrifice a sheep, because of the *Fatwa* of Ibn 'Abbas ﷺ, but his *'Umrah* is still valid.[150]

---

[150] See: *Sunan Al-Baihaqi* (5/172). Al-Albani said in *Irwa'ul-Ghalil* that it is *Sahih* and *Mawquf* (4/233). See also *Hashiyatur-Rawd* (4/54) and *Adwa'ul-Bayan* (5/389).

Whoever had intercourse before doing *Tawaf* in *'Umrah*, his *'Umrah* is invalid according to scholarly consensus. If that happened after *Tawaf* and before doing *Sa'y*, his *'Umrah* is also invalid, according to the majority. In both cases, he has to continue his *'Umrah* even though it is invalid, and he has to make it up for and offer a sacrifice (*Hady*).[151]

What the Pilgrim should do when He enters Makkah

When the pilgrim reaches Al-Masjid Al-Haram it is *Sunnah* for him to enter with his right foot first and to say:

((بِسْمِ اللهِ وَالصَّلَاةُ وَالسَّلَامُ عَلَى رسُولِ اللهِ أَعُوذُ بِاللهِ العَظِيمِ وَ بِوَجْهِهِ الْكَرِيمِ وَسُلْطَانِهِ الْقَدِيمِ مِنَ الشَّيْطَانِ الرَّجِيمِ، اللَّهُمَّ افْتَحْ لِي أَبْوَابَ رَحْمَتِكَ))

"*Bismillâh, was-salâtu was-salâm 'ala Rasulillâh, a'udhu Billâhil-'Azim wa bi wajhihil-Karim wa Sultânihil-qadim minash-Shaytanir-rajim.*[152] *Allâhummaftah li abwâba rahmatika.*

(In the Name of Allâh, and blessings and peace be upon Allâh's Messenger. I seek refuge in Allâh the Almighty and in His Noble Countenance and His Eternal Sovereignty from the accursed Satan. O Allâh, open to me the gates of Your mercy)."[153]

When he reaches the Ka'bah, he should stop reciting the *Talbiyah* before he starts *Tawaf*, if he is doing *Tamattu'* or *'Umrah*. Then he should head for the Black Stone and face it, then touch it with his right hand and kiss it. If it is too hard for him to kiss it, he should touch it with his hand or with a stick,

---

[151] *Adwa'ul-Bayan* (5/389) and *Al-Istidhkar* by Ibn 'Abdul-Barr (12/290).
[152] *Abu Dawud* (466); classed as *Sahih* by Al-Albani in *Sahih al-Jami'*.
[153] *Muslim* (713).

then kiss whatever he touched it with. If it is too difficult to touch it then he should point to it. When touching it he should say "*Allâhu Akbar*," but he should not kiss whatever he uses to point to it.

He should do seven circuits of *Tawaf*, walking at a fast pace with short steps (*Raml*) in the first three circuits that is in *Tawaf Al-Qudum*, and walking in the last four circuits. Each circuit should start and end at the Black Stone. It is *Mustahab* for him to wear his *Rida'* (upper garment) with the middle beneath his right arm and the ends over his left shoulder in all the circuits of this *Tawaf*, but not at other times. If he is not sure how many circuits he has done, he should act according to what is certain, which is the lesser number. So, if he is not sure whether he has done five or six circuits, he should assume it is five and continue on that basis. After completing this *Tawaf* he should adjust his *Rida'*, putting it over his shoulders with both edges over his chest, before praying the two *Rak'ahs* following *Tawaf*. At the time of *Tawaf*, he should be in a state of purity (*Taharah*) free of all impurities. It is *Mustahab* to recite a lot of *Adhkar* (remembrance of Allâh) and *Du'a* (supplications) during *Tawaf*, but there is no specific *Du'a* for *Tawaf* or for *Sa'y*. As for the innovation adopted by some people of reciting a specific *Du'a* for each circuit of *Tawaf*, there is no basis for this. When he comes parallel with the Yemeni Corner he should touch it with his right hand and say, "*Bismillâh wa Allâhu Akbar*," but he should not kiss it. If it is too hard for him to touch it, he may omit it and continue with his *Tawaf*, and he should not point to it or say "*Allâhu Akbar*" when he comes parallel to it. It is *Mustahab* to say between the Yemeni Corner and the Black

History of Makkah **145**

Stone:

﴿ رَبَّنَآ ءَاتِنَا فِى ٱلدُّنْيَا حَسَنَةً وَفِى ٱلْأَخِرَةِ

حَسَنَةً وَقِنَا عَذَابَ ٱلنَّارِ ﴾ [البقرة: ٢٠١]

"Our Lord! Give us in this world that which is good and in the Hereafter that which is good, and save us from the torment of the Fire!" [Al-Baqarah 2:201][154]

Every time he comes in line with the Black Stone, he should touch it and kiss it, and say, "Allâhu Akbar." If he cannot touch it or kiss it, then he should point to it each time he comes in line with it and say that.

There is nothing wrong with doing *Tawaf* from beyond Zamzam, for the entire Mosque is the place of *Tawaf*. If a person does *Tawaf* in the porticos of the Mosque, that is fine, but doing *Tawaf* nearer to the Ka'bah is preferable. When he finishes *Tawaf*, he should offer two *Rak'ahs* behind the Station of Ibrahim (*Maqam Ibrahim*), if he can do so; if it is not easy for him to do so because the place is too crowded etc., then he may offer the two *Rak'ahs* in any spot of the Mosque. It is *Sunnah* to recite *Surat Al-Fatihah* (1) and *Surat Kafirun* (109) in the first *Rak'ah*, and *Surat Al-Fatihah* and *Surat Al-Ikhlas* (112) in the second. Then it is *Mustahab* to go to Zamzam and drink from it and pour some of its water over the head, because the Prophet ﷺ did that. Then he should go to the Black Stone and touch it with his right hand, if he is able to do so, following the example of the Prophet ﷺ. Then he should go out to As-Safa through the appropriate gate and climb it or stand beside it – climbing is preferable if

---

[154] *Ahmad* (3/11), *Ibn Khuzaimah* and *Abu Dawud*; classed as *Hasan* by Al-Albani in *Sahih Abi Dawud* (1/354).

one is able to do it – and recite the words:

﴾ إِنَّ ٱلصَّفَا وَٱلْمَرْوَةَ مِن شَعَآئِرِ ٱللَّهِ ﴿ [البقرة:١٥٨].

"Verily, As-Safa and Al-Marwah (two mountains in Makkah) are of the Symbols of Allâh…" [*Al-Baqarah* 2:158]

It is *Mustahab* to face the *Qiblah* and praise and magnify Allâh, and to say:

((لاَ إِلَهَ إِلاَّ اللهُ وَاللهُ أَكْبَرُ، لاَ إِلَهَ إِلاَّ اللهُ وَحْدَهُ لاَ شَرِيكَ لَهُ، لَهُ الْمُلْكُ وَلَهُ الْحَمْدُ يُحْيِي وَيُمِيتُ وَهُوَ عَلَى كُلِّ شَيْءٍ قَدِيرٌ، لاَ إِلَهَ إِلاَّ اللهُ وَحْدَهُ، أَنْجَزَ وَعْدَهُ، وَنَصَرَ عَبْدَهُ، وهَزَمَ الأَحْزَابَ وَحْدَهُ))

"*Lâ ilâha illallâh, wallâhu Akbar. Lâ ilâha illallâhu wahdahu lâ sharika lahu, lahul-mulku wa lahul-hamdu, yuhyi wa yumitu, wa Huwa 'ala kulli shay'in Qadeer. Lâ ilâha illallâhu wahdahu, anjaza wa'dahu, wa nasara 'abdahu, wa hazamal-Ahzâba wahdahu.*

(None has the right to be worshipped but Allâh, and Allâh is the Most Great. None has the right to be worshipped but Allâh Alone with no partner or associate; to Him belong all praise and dominion, He gives life and causes death, and He has power over all things. None has the right to be worshipped but Allâh Alone, He fulfilled His Promise, He granted victory to His slave and He alone defeated the Confederates)."[155]

Then he should supplicate, raising his hands, repeating this

---

[155] *Muslim* (1218).

Dhikr and *Du'a* three times. Then he should come down and walk towards Al-Marwah, until he reaches the first green marker, whereupon men should walk quickly until they reach the second green marker, but walking quickly is not prescribed for women.

Then he should walk and climb Al-Marwah or stand there – but climbing is preferable if one is able to do it – and say and

do the same things at Al-Marwah as he did at As-Safa.

Then he should come down, and walk where he should walk and walk quickly where he should walk quickly, until he comes back to As-Safa. He should do that seven times; going counts as one and coming back counts as one. It is *Mustahab* to recite a lot of *Dhikr* and *Du'a* during *Sa'y*, and to be in a state of purity (*Taharah*) free of any impurity, but if a person does *Sa'y* without being in a state of purity, it is acceptable. Similarly, if a woman's period begins or she starts to bleed following childbirth after completing *Tawaf*, and she does *Sa'y*, that is acceptable, because purity is not a condition of *Sa'y*, rather it is *Mustahab*, as stated above.

When the pilgrim has completed *Sa'y*, he should shave his head or cut his hair. Shaving is preferable in the case of men, but if he cuts his hair and leaves shaving for when he has completed his *Hajj*, that is fine. If his arrival in Makkah is close to the time of *Hajj*, then it is preferable for him to cut his hair (upon completing *'Umrah*), and he may shave the rest of his head after *Hajj*. It is essential to cut hair from all over the head; cutting from part of the head is not good enough, just as shaving part of the head is not good enough. If the person in *Ihram* does what is mentioned, then he has completed his *'Umrah* and it becomes permissible for him to do everything that was prohibited to him during *Ihram*, unless he has brought the *Hady* (sacrificial animal) with him from outside the sanctuary, in which case he must remain in *Ihram* until he exits the *Ihram* of both *Hajj* and *'Umrah* together after completing the *Hajj*.

In the case of one who enters *Ihram* for *Hajj* only (*Ifrad*) or for *Hajj* and *'Umrah* together, it is *Sunnah* for him to exit the

Ihram of his *'Umrah* and to do the same as those who are doing *Tamattu'*, unless he has brought the *Hady* (sacrificial animal) with him, because this is what the Prophet ﷺ told his Companions to do, and he said:

"If I had not brought the *Hady* with me, I would have exited *Ihram*."[156]

If a woman starts her period or starts to bleed following childbirth after she has entered *Ihram* for *'Umrah*, she should not do *Tawaf* around the Ka'bah or do *Sa'y* between As-Safa and Al-Marwah, until she becomes pure. When she becomes pure, she should do *Tawaf* and *Sa'y*, and cut her hair, thus completing her *'Umrah*. If she does not become pure before the day of *Tarwiyah* (the eighth of Dhul-Hijjah, when the pilgrims go out to Mina), she should enter *Ihram* for *Hajj* from the place where she is staying and go out with the people to Mina – that means that she is joining her *Hajj* and *'Umrah* in *Qiran*, and she should do what the other pilgrims do, namely standing in 'Arafat and at *Al-Mash'ar Al-Haram*, stoning the *Jamarat*, staying overnight in Muzdalifah and Mina, offering the sacrifice and cutting her hair. Then when she becomes pure, she should do *Tawaf* around the Ka'bah and do *Sa'y* between As-Safa and Al-Marwah – and one *Tawaf* and one *Sa'y* will be sufficient for both her *Hajj* and *'Umrah*, because of the *Hadith* of 'Aishah 🐘 which narrates that her period came after she had entered *Ihram* for *'Umrah*, so the Prophet ﷺ said to her:

"Do what the pilgrims do but do not do *Tawaf* until you become pure."[157]

---

[156] *Al-Bukhari* (2505, 2506).
[157] *Al-Bukhari* (1650) and *Muslim* (1211).

When a menstruating woman stones the *Jamrah* on the Day of Sacrifice and cuts her hair, it then becomes permissible for her to do everything that was forbidden to her in *Ihram*, such as wearing perfume etc., except for intercourse, as is the case with other women who are pure (not menstruating). When she has done *Tawaf* and *Sa'y* after she becomes pure, then it

becomes permissible for her to have intercourse with her husband.

As-Safa and Al-Marwah, and the ruling about *Sa'y* between them

The ruling according to the majority of scholars is that *Sa'y* is a pillar of *Hajj*, without which *Hajj* is incomplete.

The conditions of *Sa'y* are:

1. Intention.
2. It should be done after a correct *Tawaf*.
3. It should start at As-Safa and end at Al-Marwah.
4. It should be done seven times.
5. The *Sa'y* should be done in the well-known *Mas'a* (place of *Sa'y*).

The *Sunnahs* of *Sa'y* are:

1. It should be done straight after *Tawaf*, unless one has an excuse.
2. Climbing up on As-Safa and Al-Marwah, reciting *Lâ ilâha illallâh* and *Allâhu Akbar*.
3. Walking as fast as possible between the two green markers – this applies to men only, not women – and walking normally elsewhere.

Going out to Mina

On the eighth day of Dhul-Hijjah – *Yaumut-Tarwiyah* – it is *Mustahab* for those in Makkah who are not in *Ihram* and those among its inhabitants who want to do *Hajj* to enter *Ihram* from their residences. It is *Mustahab* to take a bath (*Ghusl*) and to put on perfume when entering *Ihram* for *Hajj*. Then after entering *Ihram* it is *Sunnah* to head for Mina before the sun reaches its zenith or afterwards, and to recite the *Talbiyah* a great deal, and to pray *Zuhr*, *'Asr*, *Maghrib*, *'Isha'* and *Fajr* in Mina, shortening the prayers which may be shortened, namely the four-*Rak'ah* prayers. The people who live in Makkah should also shorten their prayers like other people.

Going out to 'Arafat

After the sun rises on the following day – i.e., the day of *'Arafah* – the pilgrims should set out from Mina to 'Arafat. It is *Sunnah* to stop in Namirah until noon, if possible, then to pray *Zuhr* and *'Asr*, shortened and joined together, at the time of *Zuhr*, with one *Adhan* and two *Iqamahs*. It is *Sunnah* for the *Imam* to give a *Khutbah* (sermon) before this prayer, in

which he should explain what is prescribed for the pilgrims and tell the people to fear Allâh and to adhere to His Book and the *Sunnah* of His Messenger ﷺ.

After the prayer, the people should stand in 'Arafat. All of 'Arafat is the place of standing, except for the valley of 'Uranah. It is *Mustahab* to face the *Qiblah* and Jabalur-Rahmah (the Mount of Mercy), but if it is not possible to face them both then one should face the *Qiblah*, even if that means not facing Jabalur-Rahmah. It is *Mustahab* for the pilgrim to strive hard in remembering Allâh, calling upon Him and beseeching Him during this standing. It is *Sunnah* to frequently repeat:

((لَا إِلَهَ إِلَّا اللهُ وَحْدَهُ لَا شَرِيكَ لَهُ، لَهُ الْمُلْكُ وَلَهُ الْحَمْدُ يُحْيِي وَيُمِيتُ وَهُوَ عَلَى كُلِّ شَيْءٍ قَدِيرٌ))

"Lâ ilâha illallâhu wahdahu, lâ sharika lahu, lahul-

mulku wa lahul-hamdu, yuhyi wa yumitu, wa Huwa 'ala kulli shay'in Qadeer.

(None has the right to be worshipped but Allâh Alone with no partner or associate; to Him belong all praise and dominion, He gives life and causes death, and He has power over all things)."

There are many *Du'as* that have been narrated from the Prophet ﷺ and are to be found in the books of *Du'a.*

What is meant by standing in 'Arafat

What is meant by standing in 'Arafat is standing, if only for a moment with the intention of standing, whether one actually stands or sits or rides, and whether one is aware of its significance or not, and one does that at the time of standing, from noon on the ninth of Dhul-Hijjah until the dawn on the tenth.

Rulings

It is a pillar of *Hajj* according to scholarly consensus, and *Hajj* is not complete without it. Whoever misses the standing in 'Arafat, should change his *Hajj* to *'Umrah,* then he does not have to do the things that come after the standing, such as staying overnight in Muzdalifah and Mina, and stoning the *Jamarat.* So, he should do *Tawaf* and *Sa'y* and cut his hair or shave his head. He has to make up for the *Hajj* that he has missed, even if it was a *Nafl* (voluntary) *Hajj,* and he has to offer the *Hady* (sacrifice) – by sacrificing a sheep. Whoever cannot find a sheep to sacrifice has to fast for three days during *Hajj* and seven days when he returns to his family.

The conditions of standing in 'Arafat

There are conditions of standing in 'Arafat, some of which have to do with the place and others which have to do with the time and with the person who is standing.

1. The place: The scholars are agreed that all of 'Arafat, with its boundaries that are marked nowadays by signs, is the place of standing. Wherever a person stands within that area, his *Hajj* is valid.

The valley of 'Uranah is not part of 'Arafat, so it is not valid to stand there.

2. The time: The time for standing begins at noon on the day of *'Arafah*, according to the sound opinion, and continues until dawn on the tenth of Dhul-Hijjah. Whoever stands during the day, must stay there until sunset; and whoever stands at night, even a moment is sufficient for him, because the Prophet ﷺ said:

> "Whoever reaches 'Arafat at night, has caught up with the *Hajj*."[158]

Departing to Muzdalifah and spending the Night there

When the sun sets on the day of *'Arafah*, the pilgrims have to leave for Muzdalifah, in a calm and dignified manner, reciting the *Talbiyah* a great deal. They should travel quickly through if it is possible, because that is what the Prophet ﷺ did. It is not permissible to leave before sunset.

When they reach Muzdalifah, they should offer the *Maghrib* prayer with three *Rak'ahs* and *'Isha'* with two *Rak'ahs*,

---

[158] *Al-Mulakhkhasul-Fiqhi* by Dr. Salih Al-Fawzan (1/303, 304). See also *Sahih An-Nasa'i* (3016).

putting them together with one *Adhan* and two *Iqamahs*, whether they reach Muzdalifah at the time of *Maghrib* prayer or after the time for *'Isha'* has begun. Some pilgrims go to gather the pebbles to stone the *Jamarat* as soon as they arrive, before they pray, but there is no basis for doing so. The Prophet ﷺ did not command that pebbles should be picked up for him until after he had left *Al-Mash'ar Al-Haram*. The pilgrims should spend this night in Muzdalifah, but it is permissible for the weak, such as women, children, etc., to set out in the latter part of the night, but it is confirmed that other pilgrims should stay there until they offer *Fajr* prayer, then they should stand at *Al-Mash'ar Al-Haram*, facing the *Qiblah* and reciting a lot of *Dhikr* and *Du'a*, until it has become very bright. Wherever they stand in Muzdalifah, that is good enough; they do not have to be close to *Al-Mash'ar Al-Haram* or to climb it, because the Prophet ﷺ said:

((وَقِفْتُ هَهُنَا- يَعْنِي عَلَى الْمَشْعَرِ - الْمُزْدَلِفَةُ كُلُّهَا مَوْقِفٌ))

"I stood here (meaning on the *Mash'ar*) and all of *Jam'* is a place of standing."[159]

Jam' is another name for Muzdalifah.

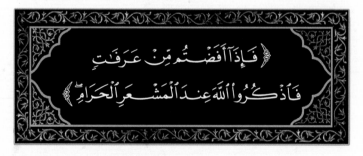

﴿ فَإِذَآ أَفَضْتُم مِّنْ عَرَفَتٍ فَٱذْكُرُوا۟ ٱللَّهَ عِندَ ٱلْمَشْعَرِ ٱلْحَرَامِ ﴾

---

[159] *Muslim* (1218) and *Sahih Ibn Khuzaimah* (2857).

Is anyone excused from staying overnight in Muzdalifah?

Yes, some people are excused from staying overnight in Muzdalifah. Those who cannot reach 'Arafat until just before dawn for some reason, such as vehicle breakdown or flight delays etc., are excused, as are those who fall sick on the night before *'Eid* and leave to seek medical treatment, and do not come back because of their sickness.

The ruling on staying overnight in Muzdalifah

The standing in Muzdalifah is obligatory, and whoever fails to do it must offer a sacrifice as expiation. Some of the scholars said that it is a pillar without which *Hajj* is incomplete, but the correct view is that it is compulsory (*Wajib*). Whoever fails to stay overnight in Muzdalifah because of an excuse, does not have to do anything and his *Hajj* is valid, but whoever does not stay overnight in Muzdalifah with no excuse, has to offer a sacrifice.

The Return to Mina

When it has become very bright, the pilgrims should set out for

Mina before the sun rises, and recite the *Talbiyah* a great deal on the way. When they reach Muhassir, it is *Mustahab* to speed up a little; and when they reach Mina near *Jamratul-'Aqabah*, they should stop reciting the *Talbiyah*. Then they should stone it when they arrive, with seven pebbles thrown one after another without interruption. The pilgrim should raise his arm when throwing, and say "*Allâhu Akbar*" with each throw. It is *Mustahab* to throw them with the Ka'bah to one's left and Mina to one's right – because this is what the Prophet 畿 did – but if a person throws them from the other sides, that is sufficient so long as the pebbles land in the place of throwing. The pebbles used to stone the *Jamarat* must be like the pebbles used in a slingshot, slightly larger than a chickpea. After stoning the *Jamrah*, he should slaughter his sacrificial animal, then shave his head or cut his hair, but shaving is preferable.

The First Stage of exiting *Ihram*

After stoning *Jamratul-'Aqabah* and shaving the head or

cutting the hair, everything that was forbidden to the pilgrim during *Ihram* now becomes permissible, except for the intercourse. This is called *At-Tahallul Al-Awwal* (the first stage of exiting *Ihram*).

Tawaf Al-Ifadah

The *Tawaf* which is done after the first stage of exiting *Ihram* is called *Tawaf Al-Ifadah* or *Tawaf Az-Ziyarah*. It is one of the pillars of *Hajj*, without which *Hajj* is incomplete.

Sa'y for those who are doing Tamattu'

After doing *Tawaf Al-Ifadah* and praying two *Rak'ahs* behind *Maqam Ibrahim*, the pilgrim should do *Sa'y* between As-Safa and Al-Marwah, if he is doing *Tamattu'*; this *Sa'y* is for his *Hajj* and his first *Sa'y* was for his *'Umrah*.

The Obligation of offering a Sacrifice (Hady) for Those doing Tamattu' and Qiran

The *Hady* is the animal from the *An'am* (cattle) – camels, cows and sheep – which the pilgrim (doing *Hajj* or *'Umrah*) offers as an act of worship to draw closer to Allâh. The pilgrim who is doing *Tamattu'* or *Qiran* and is not one of the residents of *Makkah,* must offer a sacrifice, i.e., the *Hady*, namely a sheep, or share a seventh part of a camel or a cow. That must be purchased with *Halal* wealth, because Allâh is Good and does not accept anything but that which is good.

If the pilgrim doing *Tamattu'* or *Qiran* is unable to obtain a sacrificial animal, then he must fast three days during *Hajj* and seven days after he returns to his family. He has the choice regarding the three days – he may fast them before the

day of Sacrifice, or he may fast them during the three days of *Tashriq*. Allâh says:

﴿ فَمَن تَمَتَّعَ بِٱلْعُمْرَةِ إِلَى ٱلْحَجِّ فَمَا ٱسْتَيْسَرَ مِنَ ٱلْهَدْيِ فَمَن لَّمْ يَجِدْ فَصِيَامُ ثَلَٰثَةِ أَيَّامٍ فِى ٱلْحَجِّ وَسَبْعَةٍ إِذَا رَجَعْتُمْ تِلْكَ عَشَرَةٌ كَامِلَةٌ ذَٰلِكَ لِمَن لَّمْ يَكُنْ أَهْلُهُ حَاضِرِى ٱلْمَسْجِدِ ٱلْحَرَامِ ﴾ [البقرة:١٩٦].

"And whosoever performs the *'Umrah* in the months of *Hajj*, before (performing) the *Hajj*, (i.e., *Hajj At-Tamattu'* and *Al-Qirân*), he must slaughter a *Hady* such as he can afford, but if he cannot afford it, he should observe fasts three days during the *Hajj* and seven days after his return (to his home), making ten days in all. This is for him whose family is not present at *Al-Masjid Al-Haram* (i.e., non-resident of Makkah)." [*Al-Baqarah* 2:196]

In *Sahih Al-Bukhari* it is narrated that 'Aishah and Ibn 'Umar ﷺ said:

"No dispensation was given to anyone on the days of *Tashriq* allowing them to fast, apart from those who could not afford a *Hady*." [160]

This is according to the ruling that is attributed to the Prophet ﷺ. It is preferable to observe the three days of fasting before the day of *'Arafah*, so that one will not be fasting on the day of *'Arafah*, because the Prophet ﷺ stood at 'Arafat when he was not fasting, and he forbade fasting the day of *'Arafah* in 'Arafat. It is permissible to fast the three days one after the

---

[160] *Al-Bukhari* (1997, 1998).

other or separately. Similarly, the seven days need not be fasted one after the other; it is permissible to fast them either all together or separately. It is preferable to delay fasting the seven days until one has returned to one's family, because Allâh says:

﴿ وَسَبْعَةٍ إِذَا رَجَعْتُمْ ﴾ .

"…and seven days after his return (to his home)." [Al-Baqarah 2:196]

Conditions of the *Hady*

The following conditions apply to the *Hady*:

1. It must be an animal of the *An'am* (cattle), which are in order of preference: camels, cows and sheep. One camel or cow is equivalent to seven sheep.

2. The *Hady* must be healthy and free of any faults, which would disqualify it as a sacrifice. A sick animal which is obviously sick is not acceptable, neither is a one-eyed animal which is obviously one-eyed or a lame animal which is obviously lame.

3. According to the well-known opinion, a camel should be five years old, a cow should be two years old, a goat should be one year old and a lamb should be six months old.

The Order of Rituals on the Day of Sacrifice

It is preferable that the rituals on the day of Sacrifice should be done in the following order:

1. Stoning *Jamratul-'Aqabah*.
2. Sacrifice.
3. Shaving the head or cutting the hair.
4. *Tawaf* around the Ka'bah.
5. *Sa'y* for those who are doing *Tamattu'*, and also for those who are doing *Ifrad* and *Qiran*, if they did not do *Sa'y* when they did *Tawaf Al-Qudum*.

This order is preferable, but if a person does some things before others, that is acceptable, because it is proven that the Prophet ﷺ allowed such dispensations. That includes doing *Sa'y* before *Tawaf*, as it was reported that the Prophet ﷺ was asked about someone who did *Sa'y* before *Tawaf*, and he said, "Do it, and it is fine."[161]

The Second Stage of exiting *Ihram*

We stated above that after stoning the *Jamarat* and shaving the head or cutting the hair, everything becomes permissible to the pilgrim apart from intercourse. This is called the first stage of exiting *Ihram*. When the pilgrim has stoned *Jamratul-'Aqabah* and shaved his head or cut his hair, then done *Tawaf Al-Ifadah* and *Sa'y* between As-Safa and Al-Marwah, everything then becomes permissible for him, including intercourse, and this is called the second stage of exiting *Ihram*.

---

[161] This subject is discussed in more detail in *Kitabul-Hajj wal-'Umrah waz-Ziyarah* by Shaikh Ibn Baz, and in *Bidayatul-Mujtahid* and *Al-Fiqh 'alal-Madhahibil-Arba'ah*, both by 'Abdur-Rahman Al-Jazirah. [*Translator's Note*: The book by Shaikh Ibn Baz is available in English under the title *Verifying and Explaining Many Matters of Hajj, Umrah and Ziyarah in the Light of the Qur'an and Sunnah*, published by Darussalam, Riyadh]

After exiting *Ihram*, it is *Mustahab* for the pilgrim to drink Zamzam water and to drink his fill of it, and to make whatever beneficial *Du'a* he can.[162] Al-Baihaqi reported with *Sahih Isnad* that when 'Abdullah bin Al-Mubarak drank Zamzam water, he would face the Ka'bah and say, "O Allâh, Allâh's Messenger ﷺ said: 'The water of Zamzam is for the purpose for which it is drunk,' and I am drinking it to offset thirst on the Day of Resurrection."[163]

Going back to Mina

After doing *Tawaf Al-Ifadah* and *Sa'y* – for those who have to do *Sa'y* – the pilgrims go back to Mina and stay there for three days and nights. They stone the three *Jamarat* on each day after the sun has reached its zenith. It is *Mustahab* to follow the proper sequence of stoning, starting with the first *Jamrah*, which is next to Masjid Al-Khaif, then stoning the second *Jamrah*, then the third. Stoning the *Jamarat* on the first two days of the days of *Tashriq* is compulsory (*Wajib*), as is staying overnight in Mina. After stoning the *Jamarat* on the two days mentioned, whoever wants to, can hasten to leave Mina, that is permissible; and whoever stays overnight for a third night and stones the *Jamarat* on the third day, that is preferable and brings a greater reward.

With regard to the time of stoning the *Jamarat*, the time begins after sunrise on the day of Sacrifice and lasts until sunset; on the days of *Tashriq* (11th, 12th and 13th of Dhul-

---

[162] *Al-Hajj wal-Umrah waz-Ziyarah* by Shaikh Ibn Baz (p. 47).
[163] *Shu'abul-Iman* by Al-Baihaqi (4128). See also *Izalatud-Dahsh wal-Walah* by Muhammad bin Idris Al-Qadiri (p. 162).

Hijjah), however, the time starts after the sun has reached its zenith and lasts until sunset.

The scholars – including Shaikh Ibn Baz – have issued *Fatwas* stating that it is permissible to stone the *Jamarat* at night.

It is permissible for those who are unable to do the stoning to appoint someone to do it on their behalf, subject to the condition that the person appointed as proxy should also be doing *Hajj* that year; he should throw stones on his own behalf first, then on behalf of the person who has appointed him.

Conditions of stoning the *Jamarat*

In order for the stoning of the *Jamarat* to be done correctly, the following conditions must be met:

1. There must be seven pebbles for each *Jamrah*.

2. There must be seven throws. If the pilgrim throws them

all together, or two by two, or three by three, that is not acceptable, and what he throws together is counted as one throw.

3. The stones must be thrown by his own hand if one is able to do that.

4. What is to be thrown are pebbles; one should not throw shoes, mud, metal or anything else.

5. The thrower must aim at the *Jamrah*; if he aims at anything else but hits the *Jamrah*, that is not acceptable.

6. He should make sure that his stone has fallen in the target area, even if it does not hit the pillar itself.

7. He must stone the *Jamarat* in order, starting with the small one, then the medium sized one, then *Al-'Aqabah* – the biggest one.

Some Charitable Institutions and Universities in Makkah Al-Mukarramah

Muslim World League
(Rabitatul-'Alamil-Islami)

The Muslim World League is a popular-based Islamic institution that has no connections to any government, rather it is independent and seeks to bring together all forces for good working in the Islamic world, resisting alien thoughts that are working against the beliefs and countries of the Muslims. It does not interfere in the internal matters of individual states.

It was founded in 1381 AH/1962 CE, following the first Islamic Conference in Makkah Al-Mukarramah. Its aims include the following:

1. Working to establish the rule of Islamic *Shari'ah* in Muslim countries.

2. Making the most of *Hajj* in order to spread Islamic awareness.

3. Encouraging Muslim *Da'iyahs* in all parts of the Muslim world to work in spreading Islam.

4. Spreading Islamic teachings by establishing Islamic schools and institutes throughout the world.

5. Working to spread the language of the Qur'ân.

And there are other goals.

The main bodies and councils in the Muslim World League

1. *Al-Mu'tamarul-Islami Al-'Aam*, which is the highest legislative body.

2. *Al-Majlisut-Ta'sisi*, which drafts the policies of the MWL and issues resolutions and recommendations as required.

3. *Al-Amanatul-'Aammah*, which is the executive body that directly supervises the work and activities undertaken by the MWL.

4. *Al-Majlisul-A'la Al-'Alami lil-Masajid* (for mosques).

5. The Institute for Training *Imams* and *Khatibs*.

6. The Islamic Jurisprudence (*Fiqh*) Council.

7. The Islamic Aid Agency.[164]

Charitable Organization for Memorization of the Holy Qur'ân
(Al-Jama'atul-Khairiyah litahfizul-Qur'ânil-Karim)

This charitable organization was founded in 1382 AH by a group of righteous people. The main force in its founding – after Allâh – was Shaikh Muhammad Yusuf Sayti Al-Pakistani (may Allâh have mercy on him).

The first group memorized the entire Qur'ân graduated in 1386 AH, it was a group of 18 *Hafiz*. The first *Halaqah* (study circle) was held in the mosque of Muhammad bin

---

[164] *Al-Diblomasiyah wal-Marasim Al-Malakiyah* – 'Abdur-Rahman bin Muhammad Al-Hammudi (1/680).

Ladin in Al-Hafa'ir, and the number of its members was very small, but now the number of students is more than twenty thousand, and the number of *Halaqahs* reaches into the hundreds. This organization holds more than forty *Halaqahs* in the *Haram* of Makkah.

The Darul-Arqam bin Abul-Arqam Institute belongs to this organization, to which students are admitted after having memorized the entire Qur'ân; in this institute they study for two years to master the recitation and *Tajwid* of the Qur'ân.

In this institute there is a *Halaqah* which is devoted to teach the *Qira'at* (variant reciting styles of the Qur'ân), the students join it after completing their studies in the institute, and spend three years studying the variant readings and sciences of the Qur'ân.

There are also five *Halaqahs* just for students from Muslim minorities throughout the world, and there are fourteen *Halaqahs* devoted to preparing people to teach the Qur'ân in institutes.

This organization operates under the auspices of Imam Muhammad bin Sa'ud Islamic University, and when the Ministry of *Awqaf* was established, this organization was incorporated into it.[165]

Ummul-Qura University (Jami'atu Ummil-Qura)

Ummul-Qura University is one of the universities in the Kingdom, located in Makkah Al-Mukarramah. It is an old university which started as a college of *Shari'ah* in 1369 AH.

---

[165] See *Ibhaj Al-Hâjj* by Shaikh Az-Zahrani (p. 205).

In 1391 AH, the college of *Shari'ah* was added to other colleges that were attached to King 'Abdul-'Aziz University in Jeddah.

In 1400 AH, a royal decree was issued to announce the founding of Ummul-Qura University in Makkah Al-Mukarramah. There is a large campus belonging to the University.

The University comprises a number of colleges and an institute for teaching Arabic to non-native speakers. The colleges of the university include the following:

1. The College of *Shari'ah* and Islamic Studies.
2. The College of *Da'wah* and *Usulud-Deen*.
3. The College of Education.
4. The College of Arabic Language and Literature.
5. The College of Applied Science.
6. The College of Social Science.
7. The College of Engineering Science.

The University also has a College of Education located in the city of At-Ta'if. The University also offers Master's degrees and doctorates. Many students have graduated from this university and spread throughout the world, spreading knowledge and sound belief (*'Aqidah*), fighting innovation and misguidance. *In sha Allâh*, this University will remain as a bright beacon of Islam.[166]

Darul-Hadith Al-Makkiyah

This is a school which is doing great and blessed work in

---

[166] *'Ala Tariqil-Mustaqbal – At-Ta'limul-'Aali*, Ministry of Information; *Ibhajul-Hâjj* by Shaikh Nasir bin Musfir Az-Zahrani (p. 209).

serving the Holy Qur'ân and the pure *Sunnah* of the Prophet
※. Many students from all parts of the Muslim world have
benefited from it.

It was founded in 1352 AH as a private school, then it came
under the auspices of the Islamic University of Al-Madinah
Al-Munawwarah in 1391 AH.

It is comprised of two stages:

The first is a middle school after which students are granted a
certificate. This stage lasts for three years.[167]

The second is the secondary level, lasting for three years.

Madrasah Darul-Hadith Al-Khairiyah

This is a charitable school which was founded with the
approval of King 'Abdul-'Aziz bin 'Abdur-Rahman Aal
Sa'ud (may Allâh have mercy on him) in 1352 AH. Since that
time it has continued to serve the Qur'ân and *Sunnah*. It is
supervised by a higher committee headed by the Grand
Mufti of the Kingdom of Saudi Arabia.

This school comprises four stages, which are as follows:

1. Madrasah Darul-Faizeen Al-Ibtida'iyah (elementary
   level), for teaching memorization of the Holy Qur'ân.
   This stage of study lasts for six years and is supervised by
   the Ministry of Education with regard to its educational
   aspect only. Financial and administrative matters are
   taken care of by Darul-*Hadith* Al-Khairiyah, which was
   founded in 1304 AH.

---

[167] *Ibhajul-Hâjj* by Shaikh Nasir bin Musfir Az-Zahrani (p. 213).

2. Middle school; this stage lasts for three years.

3. Secondary school; this stage lasts for four years.

4. Department of higher (post-secondary) studies. This stage lasts for four years, and students at this level are given monthly financial assistance and some other kinds of help.

Study is based on the semester system, following the academic year in the Kingdom of Saudi Arabia. The intention is that this school should be a guiding light aimed at correcting belief and enjoining what is good and forbidding what is evil, so that it will help to restore the purity of Islam and rid it of innovated matters.

Children of more than forty different nationalities from within the Muslim world and other countries study at this school. The number of students exceeds 1100.[168]

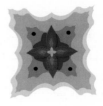

---

[168] *As-Salafiyun fil-Hind wal-Malik 'Abdul-'Aziz* by Ash-Shuway'ir.

The Most Famous Libraries in Makkah Al-Mukarramah

Maktabatul-Haramil-Makki (Library of the Makkan Sanctuary)

This is an old library which derives its importance from the importance of the Noble Sanctuary.

It includes major Islamic reference books and rare manuscripts. It opens its doors morning and evening for seekers of knowledge to benefit from it and for scholars to partake of its treasures. This library is located close to the Noble Sanctuary of Makkah.

Al-Maktabatul-'Aammah (Public Library) – belonging to the Board of Education

This is a huge library which operates under the auspices of the Board of Education. It contains a huge number of books in which the seeker of knowledge will find what he is looking for. It is located in Hayy Az-Zahir, in Makkah.

Maktabah Jami'il-Furqan

This library contains a large number of religious and cultural works. It is located in Hayy Al-'Awali. Shaikh Nasir bin Musfir Az-Zahrani says of the library:

"Students love it and scholars support it, and the people compete in supporting it. It is a beacon for *Ahlus-Sunnah*, for it contains no books of innovation,

myths or extremism."

Maktabah Jami'at Ummil-Qura

This is the University library, containing thousands of valuable books. It is a huge and comprehensive library.

Maktabah Makkah

This library contains rare manuscripts and brilliant books. Although it is a small library, it contains books and manuscripts that are of great benefit, and it offers an important service to seekers of knowledge. Maktabah Makkah is located close to the *Haram*.[169]

---

[169] *Ibhajul-Hâjj; Daurul-Mamlakatil-'Arabiyahtis-Sa'udiyah fi Khidmatil-Islam.*

Some other Historical Locations in Makkah Al-Mukarramah

There are many historical buildings in Makkah, including many mosques, some of which we have mentioned above when discussing the mosques of Makkah. Makkah also contains – because of its historical importance – many palaces and ancient houses. Some of them have unfortunately been lost due to the demands of modern development and expansion, but some of the most ancient buildings have been preserved.

Among the houses of historical significance in Makkah are the house of Abu Sufyan ﷺ, the house of Khadijah ﵂, the house of 'Abdullah bin 'Abdul-Muttalib, and the house of 'Ali bin Abi Talib ﷺ.[170]

---

[170] *As-Siyahah fil-Mamlakahtil-'Arabiyah As-Sa'udiyah* by Dr. Sultan Ahmad Ath-Thaqafi (p. 161).